Pioneering in the San Juan

Personal Reminiscences Of Work Done In
Southwestern Colorado During
The "GREAT SAN JUAN EXCITEMENT"

BY THE
REV. GEORGE M. DARLEY, D.D.

D1431630

WESTERN REFLECTIONS
PUBLISHING COMPANY®

A REPRINT BY
WESTERN REFLECTIONS PUBLISING COMPANY
LAKE CITY, COLORADO

A Reprint Published by
Western Reflections Publishing Company
P.O Box 1149
951 N. Highway 149
Lake City, Colorado 81235

www westernreflectionspub com
westref@montrose net

Printed in the United States of America

Library of Congress Number 2008923132

ISBN 978-1-932738-61-2

Prologue

George Darley was born in 1847 in Nebraska Territory. He left formal schooling at the age of fourteen to learn the carpentry trade from his father. He eventually went to Galveston, Texas, where he used his carpentry skills in lining the inside of vessels that would carry grains. It was there that he began his ministry, although, as was common in those days, he had no formal education and was not ordained

George Darley followed his brother Alexander, an ordained Presbyterian minister, to the new state of Colorado in 1876. George worked as a carpenter, while his brother did "Home Missionary Work" in the wilds of Colorado. Alexander and George lived in Del Norte, Colorado, which Alexander used as a base to do missionary work in the San Luis Valley. Alexander is credited with starting the first non-Catholic church in the San Luis Valley

Alexander and George eventually visited Lake City, Colorado, where the two brothers organized the Lake City Presbyterian Church on June 18, 1876. Lake City was only a year old, but it was growing furiously The town was not only a supply point for local mines, but was also one of the main gateways to the entire San Juan mining region As such, it gained an air of culture quickly, an important part of which was the arrival of religion

George moved his residence to Lake City in August, 1876, in order to preach and do carpentry work. His first project was to construct a church for the Presbyterians. It was finished and dedicated on November 18, 1876, and was the first church building on the Western Slope of Colorado. George also made the pews for the church out of scaffolding used in its construction. Alexander continued to work in the

San Luis Valley, but George stayed in Lake City and was later ordained.

George Darley also started the first church in Ouray, Colorado, in 1877, traveling to that town over 12,000-foot Engineer Pass with his life long friend and pioneering minister, Sheldon Jackson. Darley continued to do missionary work during the 1870s and 1880s. His wife, Emma Jean, and their two sons came to Lake City in 1877, and George built the church manse (home for the minister) Emma Jean was the first minister's wife to live on the Western Slope of Colorado

Later, George helped to start the Presbyterian College of the Southwest, a school to train Presbyterian ministers, and he either helped start or personally started numerous churches in the San Juan. One of his peers wrote that "no minister has done more for Presbyterianism in Colorado .. than Darley"

In 1899, he wrote *Pioneering in the San Juan*, detailing his exciting life during the "Great San Juan Excitement" of 1875, '76 and '77. Darley explains the different social strata in the new mining towns and the difficulties and dangers associated with traveling and surviving the bitter cold and deep snows of San Juan winters. The book also includes numerous adventures that seem incredible today, but were all in a day's work for a San Juan minister in the 1870s; and, wonderful photographs from the time that enhance the reader's understanding of America's pioneering period.

Darley died in 1917 after a vigorous and exciting life in the West. His book will always be one of the primary sources of Colorado history and, hopefully, an inspiration for today's missionaries

P David Smith
Publisher

Sincerely Yours,
Geo. M. Darley.

PIONEERING IN
THE SAN JUAN

PERSONAL REMINISCENCES OF WORK DONE IN
SOUTHWESTERN COLORADO DURING THE
"GREAT SAN JUAN EXCITEMENT"

BY THE
REV. GEORGE M. DARLEY, D.D.

"Surely there is a vein for the silver, and a place for
the gold where they find it."—*Job xxviii. 1.*

"What shall it profit a man, if he shall gain the
whole world, and lose his own soul?"—*St. Mark viii. 36.*

"Or what shall a man give in exchange for his soul?"
—*St. Mark viii. 37.*

Fleming H. Revell Company
Chicago : New York : Toronto
1899

To my Wife,

EMMA JEAN DARLEY,

WHO HAS THE HONOR OF BEING THE FIRST
MINISTER'S WIFE TO CROSS THE SIERRA
MADRE RANGE OF MOUNTAINS IN COLORADO,

THESE PAGES

Are Affectionately Dedicated.

PREFACE

This book is an attempt to present, in simple words, the reminiscences of work performed by a Presbyterian missionary, in Southwestern Colorado, during the "Great San Juan Excitement;" with the sincere desire to awaken a deeper interest in Home Missions. "Content to fill a little place, if God be glorified."

G. M. D.

CONTENTS

CONTENTS

LIST OF ILLUSTRATIONS

BEGINNING OF THE GREAT
SAN JUAN EXCITEMENT

"The Great San Juan Gold Excitement" dates back to 1874, when Enos T. Hotchkiss discovered the mine which bore his name for a number of years. Immediately upon the opening of this property, a rush was made into Lake City. This now famous mine, which lies three miles to the south of Lake City, was practically abandoned when, in 1879, Samuel Wendell relocated the property as the "Golden Fleece," and through Mr. Wendell it found its way into the hands of the present owners.

Pioneering in the San Juan

CHAPTER I

PIONEERING IN PREACHING

"As we stand and listen to a low and increasing hum,
  We hear the tramp of thousands that here in the future will
    come.
They will come for the air and sunshine,
  They will come for scenery grand,
They will come for the gold and silver,
  From every civilized land." —*Prospector.*

In this age of electricity, when men think quick, live fast and die young as a general rule, reminiscences are below par. Men prefer to look forward rather than backward. And yet we believe that it is well, at times, to take a look at the past, that we may see what progress Christianity has made in Colorado.

More than twenty-two years have passed since I began preaching the Gospel in this State; and I can truthfully say that the churches have kept pace with the material growth and the increase in population. History teaches that Christianity generally prospers in mountainous regions. The length, height, breadth and grandeur of our great mountain ranges are in perfect harmony with the rugged, grand and sublime evangelical doctrines presented by ministers of the Gospel. The great peaks remind me of many of the precious truths presented in the Bible—Pike's Peak, of comforting, strengthening, soul-cheering atonement; Sierra Blanca, of God's precious promises. At times this mountain is enveloped in dark clouds; yet they are always lifted and never mar her grandeur and beauty. So it is with God's children—dark clouds at times surround them; but these clouds are lifted by His almighty hand, and joyfully we "press toward the mark for the prize of the high calling of God in Christ Jesus."

In the spring of 1876 there was not a church building on the Pacific slope in Colorado. The first church was erected by the Presbyterians in Lake City and dedicated November 19, 1876—just five months, to a day, from the time of organization. Lake City was a "live mining-camp," largely made up of young men of that class who were willing to prospect and take all kinds of chances in order to make money; but they had no desire to work underneath the ground. Miners were scarce, while prospectors were numerous. No class of men knew better how to treat a minister they liked in a royal manner than the men who went into southwestern Colorado during the great San Juan "excitement" of '75, '76 and '77. Nor could a more intelligent, plucky, warm-hearted set of men be found; men who knew what was right.

Among them were many who had been taught in Eastern homes, by pious parents, that "man's chief and highest end is to glorify God and fully enjoy him forever." Yet strange as it now seems— when looking back to those exciting times—many of these men, from the best of homes, found their way into the large gambling-halls that were in all the camps; claiming they only wished to see what was going on and not for the purpose of taking part in the games. Yet, notwithstanding these claims, many, after getting, as they thought, "the run of the game," did "fight the tiger." Some did so successfully; others did not.

When entering camps where no religious services had been held I invariably went to the right place to find an audience; and in every case was cour-teously and kindly received and generally told: "Just wait, Brother Darley, until the games can be stopped, and we will give you a chance at the

17

FIRST CHURCH BUILT ON THE PACIFIC SLOPE IN COLORADO.

FIRST PARSONAGE BUILT ON THE PACIFIC SLOPE IN COLORADO.

boys." It was not always an easy matter to stop the games; winners were usually willing, while the losers were not. But so soon as the games closed then "roulette," "keno," "poker," and "faro" would give place for a time to the Gospel.

A more convenient pulpit than a "faro-table" could not be found; nor a more respectful and intelligent audience. In what occasional singing we did have, men with trained voices, rich and sweet, would sing without books those grand old hymns: "Jesus, Lover of My Soul" and "Rock of Ages, Cleft for Me." With bowed heads they listened to the prayer; often with tears in their eyes to the "old, old story," being told as they had heard it "back East," while sitting in a pew beside father, mother, or fond wife and dear children.

The contrast was as great between the Eastern pew and beer kegs, whisky barrels and chairs, as it was between the Eastern pulpit and a Western faro-table, behind which the minister stood; but the Christ presented was the same—and those men's souls were as dear to the Savior. In one camp I became acquainted with a "faro-dealer" who had a decidedly clerical look. His beautiful gray beard and ministerial dress added much to his elegant manners. He always called me "Brother Darley."

PIONEERING IN PREACHING

I said to a young man fresh from the East, as I met him at the door of a large gambling-hall: "Were you in the habit of entering such houses in the East?" He answered: "I was never in a saloon or gambling-house in my life until I came to this camp. My folks would be ashamed of me if they knew I frequented such places." Having hold of his hand, and the light shining in our faces, I said: "Should you be any less of a man out West than you were back East?" By the flash of his eye and the color in his face I saw that he was offended; but I held his hand and kept looking him in the eye. Finally he dropped his head and said: "I ought not to be."

One Sabbath night, after service, it became necessary for me to visit a large dance-hall located in "Hell's Acre." I there talked with young men who less than an hour before were sitting in God's house. Even amid the thunders of the coming storm, the cry was heard: "On with the dance! Let joy be unconfined!" During those years of toil, joy, sadness and rejoicing, I was often reminded of the words of the weeping Prophet: "Weep ye not for the dead, neither bemoan him; but weep sore for him that goeth away." Several times I was asked if I could afford to know so many sporting-men, and fast women. "Associations," said one sanctimonious man, "have a great deal to do with a minister's character." I replied that I believed with the old blacksmith, who said, when told that if he would associate with so and so it would give him character: "I can hammer out a better character on my anvil than any set of men can give me." If I could not know and, so far as necessary, "associate" with all classes, I was not the man for the place.

In '76 La Veta was the terminal of the Denver and Rio Grande Railroad. It was a long, hard stage ride from La Veta into the San Juan country. During the day the grandeur of the scenery would interest passengers; but through the long nights even "old timers" grew tired and, so soon as the stage struck the "Slumgullion Road," which was far from being "freighters' paradise," the driver would join with the freighters in swearing at the Mexicans to "pull out of the road." On this road there was a fall of several thousand feet in about twelve miles; and a few miles of that was corduroy. Where there was none, the freighters claimed that "every ten feet there was a stone projecting from six to eighteen inches and frequently on the opposite side a hole from six to eighteen inches deep, with a stump in the middle."

PIONEERING IN PREACHING

The Rev. Sheldon Jackson, D. D. (ex-Moderator of the General Assembly of the Presbyterian Church), once said to me, while trying to get the crooks out of his legs and rub down the lumps that had risen on different parts of his body: "Brother Darley, I have staged it all over this Western country; I have staged it through the tamarack swamps of Wisconsin; but I never staged it over such a road before." Dr. Jackson was always welcome at my mountain home, for he never growled, no matter how hard the trip. He has the pluck that I admire.

In the seventies many difficulties had to be faced in the San Juan that were more than the average minister cared to face then, or would care to face now. To go beyond Lake City meant to go where there were no bridges across streams and, in some directions, no wagon roads—only trails throughout the greater part of the San Juan, and often they were very rough, while the distance between cabins was so great that frequently the missionary had to sleep on the ground.

My walk of one hundred and twenty-five miles (more than half the distance through deep snow), in five days and four nights, is often spoken of by "old timers." All the streams had to be waded; and when I reached Ouray, with swollen limbs, nearly used up, and suffering terribly, Messrs. George A. Scott and James McDonald invited me to their cabin and, after procuring a bottle of arnica, both went to work and did all they could to limber me up. On Sabbath I was hardly able to walk, so did not preach until Thursday of the following week. The sermon was the first preached in Ouray or in the Uncompahgre region.

The first church built in Ouray, and the second on the western slope in Colorado, was a Presbyterian church, dedicated October 14, 1877. I say it, without fear of contradiction, that in no other frontier town in Colorado (Ouray is no longer a frontier town) could the same amount of money be raised more easily than that so cheerfully given by the citizens of the camp for the erection of their first house of worship.

When preparing to start home "Cap" Cline (who, with General Adams, afterwards rescued Mrs. Meeker and daughter from the White River Ute Indians) and others pled with me not to attempt to cross Engineer Mountain that day, for it was snowing hard in Ouray. But, like some other young men who lived in the San Juan at that time, my bump of caution was not very well developed, so started, and found nearly four feet of fresh snow above "timber line." Thus, walking was difficult going into Ouray to preach the first sermon—and getting out of Ouray after the first church was dedicated. It was on this trip that I lost an elegant pair of buckskin leggings.

We often speak of the rough experiences of frontier work, and of the roughness of the work itself, when compared with the smooth and more refined labor in our cities or in the old-established churches of the Eastern villages. Yet, after all, there is a sameness about the work that can be illustrated in this way. During my varied experience in Colorado I have often officiated at funerals very different in appearance. A rough box holds the body and an old wagon is the hearse; the mourners and minister follow on foot. When the place of burial is reached, the hole in the ground is uneven in width, and boulders project on the sides. When we attempt to let down the box, the grave is too small; so we lift it out and enlarge the grave. Finally the body is laid to rest, as the wind sighs among the tree tops and the mountains receive to their arms another body dear to someone.

Again, I have been called to officiate at a funeral where the casket was a rare piece of workmanship, beautiful and costly; and the floral offerings from friends expensive and appropriate; and with the Rev. John N. Freeman, D. D., to offer one of his characteristic prayers, which for the moment helped lift the dark clouds. The lovely hearse and nodding plumes, followed by a long line of carriages, were in striking contrast to the rickety old wagons behind which I have often walked. At the cemetery, the sides of the grave looked as though they had been planed; and the body of a dear friend (Arthur S. Adams) was laid to rest. Yet in both cases it was death. On rugged mountain side or in a beautiful cemetery, it is death. And so the Gospel is the same, whether preached in a gambling-hall, or in a fine church building. The Gospel is the same in all places. I believe in the depravity of the human race and I believe in the almighty power of the blood of Jesus Christ. "There is life for a look at the Crucified One," no matter by whom given or the place the penitent soul is in as he looks.

I was pastor of our church at Del Norte when the first meeting of the present Synod of Colorado was held at that place and the "Presbyterian College of the Southwest" was located. Having been president of the college as well as pastor of the church, my warmest sympathies go out toward that institution.

PIONEERING IN PREACHING

To-day our college at Del Norte is doing noble work for the Master. Rev. M. D. J. Sanchez, of whom ex-Senator Thomas M. Bowen said, while a trustee of the college, "There is a young man who is the peer of any young man of his age in Colorado," is among the first fruits of the college. Then there is Rev. A. J. Rodriguez, missionary to the Ute Indians, and many more who have graduated from the institution.

When the last day dawns and the stars fall and the heavens roll together as a scroll, it will not be the Methodists only that will be before the throne of God clothed in white, nor the Baptists nor the Presbyterians only. It will be the redeemed out of every nation and kindred and tongue and people, whose souls have been washed clean in the blood of the Lamb. Therefore, ministers of the Gospel should love all classes—the high, the lowly, the rich, the poor—keeping constantly in mind that the Lord Jesus Christ goes before us. His spirit accompanies our words and convinces men of sin, of righteousness and judgment. If we are faithful in our work we shall be richly blessed here and hereafter; for the harder we toil in the Master's vineyard now, the sweeter will be the rest in His house, by and by.

CHAPTER II

"One more unfortunate,
  Weary of breath,
  Rashly importunate,
  Gone to her death."

"Who was her father?
  Who was her mother?
  Had she a sister?
  Had she a brother?"   —*Thomas Hood.*

If all the tears shed by parents whose daughters have gone astray were bottled, they would not be greater in quantity or more bitter than the tears shed by the erring ones. The first burst of passion and excitement of a fast life soon recoil and strike the wandering one a terrible blow, bringing to the sporting-woman's heart a deep sense of the distance there is between her and what women prize most.

When asked, "Will you come to Magg Hartman's house and preach her funeral sermon?" I consented, because I believed it my duty to go wherever I was asked for the purpose of conducting funeral services. By so doing I had become acquainted with all classes.

Magg Hartman lived in "Hell's Acre," a part of

the new mining-camp largely given up to the sporting class. As I entered the house a very tall, well-
known character, who was sitting on the floor, rose
and said as he took my hand: "Well, Parson, this
is the way we all go." I replied: "Yes, we all
must die, but it depends on how we have lived,
and in whom we have believed, as to the place we
go when we die." "I guess that is so," said my
tall friend; for the man was a friend in the way of
"backing the Parson" financially and by being
accommodating in various ways.

I then stepped to the side of the coffin and looked
at Magg Hartman's more than ordinary face; for
few faces were more remarkable looking and few
lives had been stranger than that of this many-sided
woman. As the "girls" came in from the "dance-
halls" I took each one by the hand and spoke a
kind word. When all was ready for the funeral
service I noticed a strained attempt on their faces
to "take it," which plainly said: "You hold a full
hand now, so just wade in." Before the first eleven
verses of the eighth chapter of St. John had been
read, arms were unfolded and the strained look
began to leave their faces; and as words void of
severity were spoken tears began filling their eyes.
Soon every head was bowed and, had I not

witnessed such scenes before, I might have believed every one would leave the paths of sin and seek a better life.

After the pall-bearers had fastened the top on the coffin one of the "girls" asked if I would go with them to the cemetery. Her request was granted. Who can tell what impressions the reading of God's Word, and the funeral sermon, made upon the minds and hearts of those outcasts of society, many of them mere girls? Men who have seen much of life know that there are thousands of bleeding, aching and sorrowing hearts that are struggling against the terrible current of prejudice and cold-heartedness that is so prevalent; battling hard against the sense of shame in their own hearts and against the powers of a cold world; traveling in the most lonely of life's paths without one kind word to cheer, without one glimmer of light to guide their lonely footsteps until, discouraged, disheartened and crushed, these words of deepest gloom fall from their lips:

"Go to the raging sea and say be still;
Bid the wild tempest obey thy will;
Preach to the storm, and reason with despair:
But tell not Misery's child to beware."

Many are ready to cry: "It is their own fault.

The young girl or young man ought to have remained at home and been good." Friends, how do you know that it is all their own fault? Who told you so? What means have you of knowing so much? Be honest, and acknowledge that you are ignorant regarding their temptations, surroundings, education and peculiar temperaments; the promises made them and broken—made by those you are pleased to take by the hand. Then try to have enough Christian charity and hard common sense to keep you from kicking the fallen.

If the whole human race were constituted alike —all of the same temperament, all having equal advantages—then we might be able to judge all correctly; but, since there are such differences, we should be very slow in passing harsh judgment on anyone. It is well for the fallen that there are those on earth, as well as in Heaven, who can be "touched with the feeling of" their "infirmities."

I trust that all Christians, while they cannot reasonably be expected to feel as kindly toward the fallen as some do, will remember that—

> "There's no life so lone and low
>   But strength may yet be given,
> From narrowest lot on earth to grow
>   The straighter up to Heaven."

PIONEERING IN THE SAN JUAN

When Jericho was destroyed, not Rahab alone, but "all that were with her in the house" were saved, because "she did hide the messengers that were sent."

It is a blessed thing when all in the house are saved—but how often it is otherwise! This solemn and awful truth may cause some to have charity who at the present time are as devoid of it as the stones beneath our feet. The day may come when those who are rejoicing because no wanderer belongs to their family, may say, alas!—

> "From the same father's side,
>   From the same mother's knee,
> One to lone darkness and frozen tide,
>   One to the crystal sea."

CHAPTER III

"Chill airs and wintry winds, my ear
Has grown familiar with your song,"
—Longfellow.

Some years ago, while reading the "Denver Republican," I saw an article taken from the "Hinsdale Phonograph": "San Juan Weather Comparisons." In it I found the following: "While congratulating ourselves for the splendid weather San Juan is experiencing at present, we may remember that every season is not this way. In 1879 the snow was eight feet deep on the Continental Divide the last of December, and the mail from Del Norte to Lake City was carried the entire distance on sleds from November 25 to April 8, a period of almost four months and a half."

The reading of this brought to my mind, with a freshness not altogether pleasant, one of the wildest rides I ever had—and I had many a wild one during the seventies. For a month that winter no mail could be carried from Clear Creek to Powder Horn, except on a "snow-shoer's" back. One of the drivers nearly lost his life while trying to get through with a sled. A large number of men went from our camp and tried to "pack" the snow so that the mail could be brought in on sleds, but the storms were severe and the snow deep; so the plan was abandoned.

We decided that it was impossible to get papers or circulars, but letters we must have. A Swede by the name of Fjelley, one of the best "snow-shoers" in the San Juan, was employed to carry letters. He used the narrow, eleven-feet snow-shoes. I loaned him part of my "outfit," and, not being willing to accept pay for the use of it, he gave my little girl a silver dollar, which she has kept and calls her "snow-shoe dollar."

It was necessary for me to go to the railroad, which by that time was one hundred and fifteen miles from Lake City, having been built as far as Alamosa. But, before the headwaters of the Rio Grande could be reached, the great Sierra Madre range of mountains and the Continental Divide had to be crossed. I asked the stage agent when he thought an attempt would be made to cross the range with horses and sleighs. He said he would let me know as soon as it was decided to make the attempt. Soon after he told me: "You can keep

A WILD RIDE

it to yourself, for several want to go, and we cannot take them, for the chances are we won't get through; the drivers say 'Darley can go.' We are going to try it with two light sleighs; one span of horses to each. Be ready at midnight, when the crust on the snow will be hard."

At midnight we started—John King and myself in the front sleigh and Charlie Swift in the other. We had traveled less than two miles when the sleigh we were in upset and spilled us out. King clung to the lines, while I rolled down the side of the mountain and landed against a tree. In the upset our glass stage lamps were broken and we were left in the dark. Charlie Swift had the laugh on us. By daylight we were at Powder Horn Station, near which, in after years, proved to be a favorite place for "road agents" to collect toll from travelers. After a good breakfast and considerable conjecturing about our ever reaching Clear Creek Station, we started on the wildest ride I ever had. We fairly flew. The gulches were filled with snow and the rocks were covered; in many places the trees were snowed under. We had plenty of room and downgrade most of the way. "Talk about horses!" the driver said, "those grays would be human if they could talk." It did seem to me that they understood every word King said to them while they were being "hooked up"; for evidently they realized just what they were to do. No whip was needed to urge them to their best. "Barlow and Sanderson" never had finer horses on any of their great western stage lines. Whenever the horses' feet broke through the crust they would gather themselves for a fresh spring and, quick as a flash, dart ahead. The driver understood the horses, the horses understood the driver, and all knew the danger. I had many a wild ride in the mountains of the San Juan, but never anything to equal that one. By taking my chances that night with the drivers, I was "billed" through to Del Norte free.

Traveling in the San Juan, during the years of staging, was not considered a great pleasure by many, partly on account of the roughness of the roads and partly on account of the peculiarities of the Mexican freighters. They invariably camped in the road, and it was amusing, whenever one of their wagons would get "stuck," to see a driver running around it to turn his cattle one way, then in front of the "leaders" to turn them the other way. A Mexican does not drive cattle like an American—by keeping on one side and using a long whip. In addition to corduroy, holes, stones, stumps, steep grades and mud, many of the roads were "sidling" and the curves very sharp, so that four horses were all that could be handled by a stage-driver. One night I was in a stage-coach with thirteen other victims. The lower part of the "boot" and the back part of the coach were filled with mail. With such a heavy load the driver and express-messenger claimed that the brakes could not hold. If there was a big dance in the camp, the brakes would not work, or else were not sufficient to hold the coach. Some were uncharitable enough to say that Charlie Swift wished to get in ahead of time to attend the ball. On the night to which I refer, Charlie declared that it would be unsafe to try to hold the horses. So they went down-grade on a swinging lope, while the passengers held on and "let her go."

CHAPTER IV

"I've heard bells chiming
Full many a clime in,
Falling sublime in
   Cathedral shrine,
While at a glib rate
Brass tongues would vibrate;
But all this music
   Spoke not like thine."
   —*Father Prout* (Francis Mahony).

For aught we know to the contrary, everything
that leads men to God's house may be a part of His
plan for the winning of souls to himself; although it
be nothing more than a church bell. Anything that
helps a man's thoughts to turn toward home and
good influences, when he is far from home, proves a
blessing. All that leads man to call to mind hal-
lowed associations does him good. Man is said to
be a "religious animal." Apart from the influences
of religion and home he would soon become a wild
animal; for it is under the teachings, and by the
power of the religion of Jesus Christ, and the hal-
lowed surroundings of Christian homes that we are
lifted up and our affections purified. Without these

things an individual, family, community or nation would sink. Many who appear to appreciate home ties claim that none are benefited by Christianity; but I question if they believe it.

The mountain towns in Colorado are not free from this class, but have a large number of men professing to hold views contrary to what the Christian religion teaches. What we call "bold infidelity" shows itself plainly where it is not policy to remain covered; and in no region can we find men who are so indifferent to religious influence as in new mining-camps. Yet this class like to see "improvements in the camp," and often lend a helping hand.

After our church was built in Lake City, it being the first one on the Pacific slope in Colorado, saint and sinner expressed themselves as being very proud of it; and showed their appreciation by attending services and "paying for their preaching." Still, one important thing was lacking. Nowhere in Colorado, west of the Sierra Madre range of mountains, was there a bell of any kind for public use larger than a dinner bell. One day, to my great joy, Mr. Theodore Little, Jr., informed me that his father, Mr. Theodore Little, Sr., of Morristown, New Jersey, had bought a bell for our church—and would "pay the freight." When a man said "pay the freight,"* in those days, it often meant a great deal more than the first cost. The bell was freighted in a wagon across two great mountain ranges—the Sangre de Cristo and the Sierra Madre—also over the Continental Divide.

The bell was presented to our church in 1877. Often, during the early days of that camp, men have said after church services: "As we came toward the camp we heard the sound of a church bell and were surprised; for we had no idea that there was a church in Lake City." It no doubt reminded many of home and loved ones far away, when they heard the peals of that bell ringing out an invitation to enter God's house. It could be heard for miles and the grand old mountains seemed to take up the sound and pass it on. Since then that bell has called many to the house of prayer, who without it would never have known that there were church services in the camp—and not until the last day shall we know how great its influence for good may have been.

Years after the Lake City church was built, I was busy erecting the one at Del Norte, when United States Senator Thomas M. Bowen said to me:

---

* Some very amusing stories were told about merchants claiming that the high price of everything in which they dealt was on account of "freight being so high." Even needles cost ten times what they did "back East," because "freight was so high." ·

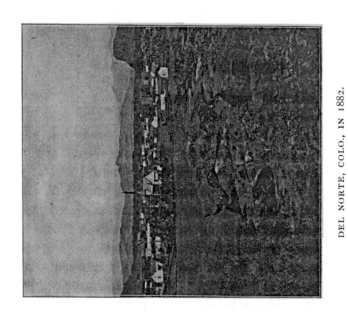

DEL NORTE, COLO., IN 1882.

LAKE CITY, COLO., IN 1877.

CHURCH BELLS

"Brother Darley, order any kind of a bell you desire for your beautiful new church and bring me the bill." We appreciated his generosity, for he had already contributed liberally toward the building. The bell, without any fixtures, weighed 734 pounds and was the finest bell in southwestern Colorado. It was cast in Troy, New York. Without the Senator's knowledge, I had his name and date of presentation cast on the bell. The Presbyterian College of the Southwest used it as well as the church. I regret to say that when the building burned, November 25, 1893, the bell was destroyed.

CHAPTER V

LOST ON THE RANGE

"I am not a little sunburnt by the glare of life, but weather-beaten by its storms." —*Stephen A. Douglas.*

After sending an account of my experience on the range to the Rev. Sheldon Jackson, D. D., he wrote the following, which appeared in the "Rocky Mountain Presbyterian" and was copied by many American and European papers:

"The esprit de corps of the Presbytery of Colorado is very great. [We had but one Presbytery at that time.] With a laudable ambition to carry the Gospel to the most distant centers of coming influence, it stops at no undertaking, however difficult or dangerous, whenever the interests of the church are concerned. And by indomitable energy, endurance and courage seeming impossibilities have been overcome.

"During the meeting of the spring Presbytery it was deemed expedient that the services at Silverton, which were suspended last fall, should be resumed at an early day. Rev. George M. Darley, of Lake City, was requested to take the matter in charge.

LOST ON THE RANGE

"Two hundred and twenty miles by rail and one hundred and seventy miles by stage brought him from the Presbytery to his mountain home. Securing a horse he started on the 17th of May, 1877, to cross the summit of the great Sierra Madre range. Slowly toiling up the valley of the Lake Fork of the Gunnison, with the wind hourly increasing in strength, he reached Lake San Christoval, 9,000 feet above the sea, to encounter a driving snow-storm.

"On and upward through the storm until, with frozen face and benumbed limbs, he reached a miner's cabin and, going in to warm, found a Presbyterian family who insisted on his remaining all night. At four o'clock the next morning he was again in the saddle, facing the great snow-crest of the continent which loomed far above him. Before accomplishing a mile the storm, which had subsided in the night, was upon him again with double fury.

"After an hour's climbing a welcome cabin afforded him breakfast. While there Gus Talbot, who carries the mail over the mountains on snow-shoes and has seen a hundred avalanches thunder and crash across his trail, came along with the mail, having traveled sixteen miles since one o'clock that morning. By seven a. m. they had reached Burrows Park, ten thousand five hundred feet above the sea. This was as far as they could ride. From there on they must walk on snow-shoes. At the park were a number of miners waiting to cross the range, but, as the storm was still raging, none of them dared make the attempt. A consultation was had. It seemed madness to venture. But the mail-carrier was determined to make the attempt, and Mr. Darley caught the spirit. Said he: 'Darley, I have carried the mail across here for years. Again and again have I crossed when I could not see as far as the point of my snow-shoe. You have faced the storm twenty-two miles yesterday, dare you face it twenty-three miles farther with me?'

"With the great calmness of men who understood the perils before them, they started—Gus Talbot with forty pounds of mail on his back and Mr. Darley with his blankets.

"Three miles brought them above timber-line. The snow-clouds drifted and surged around them. Every landmark was hidden. It seemed as if they were off in space with nothing in sight except the snow at their feet. On they plunged into that space, every few minutes stopping to gain breath.

LOST ON THE RANGE

"At length they knew that they were descending, and supposed that they had turned the summit. But soon their hopes were dashed by coming to an ascent again. Knowing that something was wrong, they turned to the left, and soon crossed their own track, and the horrible suspicion began to dawn upon them that they were lost. For three hours they had been plunging forward, unable to see anything before or around them. Fifteen minutes (it seemed hours) later and they again crossed their track, and the dread suspicion became a certainty. They were lost! Oh that the clouds would open one half second so that they could catch a glimpse of some landmark! But impenetrable clouds still enveloped them. Knowing that their only hope was to descend, they turned in their tracks and started downward. Soon they were conscious of a rapid descent, when all at once the mail-carrier dropped from view—gone over a precipice! With horror Mr. Darley sprang to one side as a great cake of snow gave way under his feet and followed the mail-carrier below. For a moment he seemed paralyzed; his heart seemed to cease to beat. Gathering up his consciousness, he at once started to the rescue. Groping his way around to the base of the cliff he found Mr. Talbot crawling out of the snow with the mail bags still on his back. The snow had broken the fall and saved his life. With great thankfulness they started on again. Soon a dim, dark line was seen below them, and the glad cry burst forth—'The timber! The timber!'

"With new energy they pressed forward and were soon sheltered from the storm in the pines, under which they lunched on a couple of biscuits. Half an hour later they are at the mining-town of Animas Forks—saved! The storm was still severe in their faces. Silverton was still fourteen miles away, and their trail led across the track of many an avalanche. But so much greater were the dangers through which they had passed, that the rest of the way seemed easy. After a good meal they started down the Animas and made Silverton that night.

"The next day Gus Talbot, the plucky mail-carrier, told the people that they could 'tie to George M. Darley, for, out of more than one hundred men he had piloted across the range, the Presbyterian preacher was the only one that had the grit to keep with him all the way.'

"But I hear one and another of my readers saying, 'want of judgment,' 'foolish,' 'mistaken zeal,' etc. It is very easy, in a comfortable home or under other circumstances, to criticise and judge what you would or would not do, but we who are on the frontier know that if the Church would do her duty and give the Gospel to the 'regions beyond' now, as in the days of the apostles and martyrs, some of her ministers must needs face physical hardships and sufferings and dangers like the shipwreck and stonings and beatings and perils of Paul. The men that observe the wind and regard the clouds and consult their comfort are not the men for the front. We need sterner material. We need men that can endure hardness, face dangers, take the chances, attempting seeming impossibilities, not counting even their lives dear unto them, if thereby the Church can be advanced. And the Church should thank God that she has a ministry willing to do this work. All honor to the pioneers of the Church. "

CHAPTER VI

A DEAD FARO—DEALER

"The saint who enjoyed the communion of heaven,
 The sinner who dared to remain unforgiven;
 The wise and the foolish, the guilty and just,
 Have quietly mingled their bones in the dust."

—Thomas Hood.

'To live uprightly is sure the best,
 To save ourselves, and not to damn the rest."

—Dryden.

An out-and-out manly Christian—one who believed
that Christianity is the backbone of the highest type
of manhood; one whose only fear was to do wrong;
one who was always ready to render assistance to
the needy, or to those in danger—had the respect of
every man in the camp, whether he was a Christian
or a faro-dealer; while those who were continually
offering the Pharisee's prayer, holding on to the
almighty dollar and making excuses for not step-
ping to the front when either distress or danger
called, were heartily despised. Whenever one of
these Pharisaical creatures came to me bemoaning
the wickedness of our camp, and saying, "It is

unwise to spend time trying to reach the sporting
fraternity, they are so bad,'' these words of Robert
Burns would come to my mind:

> "My son, these maxims make a rule
>   And lump them aye thegither;
> The rigid righteous is a fool,
>   The rigid wise anither;
> The cleanest corn that e'er was dight
>   May have some pyles o' chaff in;
> So ne'er a fellow creature slight
>   For random fits o' daffin.''

No good citizen has any defense to make or
apologies to offer for wrong-doing. Yet every
Christian, while hating sin, should love the sinner.
Association with all classes during the San Juan
excitement taught me that many of the reckless
class, notwithstanding their faults, were neither
narrow-minded nor selfish. Though they gave from
impulse, rather than principle, they were often
very generous; not to their friends only, but also to
a fallen foe.

I know that good people consider a "faro-dealer"
"a very bad man." This is true in part. It
depends on what we mean by "a very bad man."
If we look at a faro-dealer from a Christian standpoint he is certainly "a very bad man." If we

47

consider him from a good citizen's standpoint he is just as bad. But, looking at him from the standpoint of fair-dealing, "outside his faro-dealing," and the way a faro-dealer may treat a man when he is down, or the way such men often respond when asked to aid the poor whom they have never met—then, for the time being, they are not "very bad men."

When it was known that "Ben" House had died at the "San Juan Central," a large adobe dance-hall, many said: "Ben was one of the best-hearted boys in the camp." Among those generally called the "boys" a feeling existed peculiar to that class and soon manifested itself. They decided that "Ben" having been engaged in a public business—although the kind of place in which he died was not in keeping with a great display at his funeral—the stores ought to be closed during the funeral services, and that "just as good a send off ought to be given Ben as possible."

After most of the preliminaries had been arranged, "Big Hank," one of Ben's intimate friends, came and stood by the remains, and as tears coursed down his cheeks he gave me a very glowing description of the departed. What "nerve," what "generosity," how no man could "ever get Ben to

DEALING FARO IN A SAN JUAN GAMBLING HALL.

A DEAD FARO–DEALER

go back on a friend, no matter how tight a place
that friend was in." This eulogy was interspersed
with all the oaths "Big Hank" could call to mind,
when so filled with grief. He swore just to be
emphatic. If one man in that camp "swore by
note," "Big Hank" was the man. As he finished
eulogizing his dead friend, I noticed two "girls"
from one of the dance-halls coming into the building. (The remains had been carried to a hall on the
main street.) I knew they were coming to pay their
respects to "Ben." One was a tall woman, known
as "Sorrel Top," on account of the color of her hair;
the other a short, thick-set Mexican. To my sur-
prise "Big Hank" was angry, and would not permit
either of the "girls" to look at "Ben." Turning to
me, he said: "I tell you, Mr. Darley, we are going
to have a decent funeral out of this, and none of
that crowd can come near Ben now." But I
differed with him about who should come "near Ben
now," so sent him to get something that was
needed, and while he was away invited both "girls"
to look at "Ben." They were not devoid of feeling
or tenderness. The woman's heart was not entirely
gone; and a few kind words were appreciated.
Having seen much of life, my heart often warms
with sympathy for the fallen.

49

PIONEERING IN THE SAN JUAN

Robert Burns was a good judge of human nature, and no doubt was conscious that his prayer in the prospect of death would strike a responsive chord in many hearts:

"O Thou unknown Almighty, cause
　　Of all my hope and fear,
　In whose dread presence, ere an hour,
　　Perhaps, I must appear;

"If I have wandered in those paths
　　Of life I ought to shun;
　As something, loudly, in my breast,
　　Remonstrates I have done;

"Thou know'st that Thou hast form'd me
　　With passions wild and strong;
　And listening to their witching voice
　　Has often led me wrong.

"Where human weakness has come short,
　　Or frailty stept aside,
　Do Thou, All Good, for such thou art
　　In shades of darkness hide.

"Where with intention I have err'd,
　　No other plea I have,
　But, Thou art good, and goodness still
　　Delighteth to forgive."

A DEAD FARO-DEALER

I have frequently thought how little we know of what goes on between the soul of a wandering one and their God, when they are brought face to face with death; what cries for mercy may ascend to God, who sent his only Son into this sin-cursed world to seek after and "to save that which was lost." How, in such an hour, memory's pages may be revealing again to the wanderer what was written thereon in childhood's happy days by pious parents; and although covered many years by the rubbish of sin, it is not impossible for God's Spirit to touch the heart and turn the prodigal one to genuine repentance, thus leading him to seek salvation through the merits of a crucified and risen Redeemer. We have the immutable Word of the living God for it that even the brands plucked from the burning shall be saved. "Come now and let us reason together, saith the Lord; though your sins be as scarlet, they shall be as white as snow; though they be red like crimson, they shall be as wool." God forbid that anyone should be able to truthfully say, "No man cares for my soul."

"Then gently scan your brother man,
  Still gentler sister woman;
 Though they may gang a kenning wrang,
  To step aside is human;

One point must still be greatly dark,
   The reason why they do it;
And just as lamely can we mark
   How far perhaps they rue it.

"Who made the heart, 'tis he alone
   Decidedly can try us;
   He knows each chord—its various bias;
Then at the balance let's be mute,
   We never can adjust it;
What's done we partly may compute,
   But know not what's resisted."

CHAPTER VII

"There is in every human being, however ignoble, some
hint of perfection, some one place where, as we may fancy, the
veil is thin which hides the divinity behind it."
—*Confucian Classics.*

Intemperance is the greatest curse in our beloved
land. Whenever "a temperance wave" strikes us it
seems to strike all over. What is known as the
"Murphy Movement" struck our camp soon after
the movement was started. "The boys" being
hard-up for cash that winter, we knew that many
would most likely be willing to "swear off" for a
time, possibly until the snow began to melt in the
spring.

When that time came and another "boom" began,
we felt confident that a goodly number, if many
should sign the pledge, would "swear on again."
Still, a few months' respite from drink would do them
good. Therefore we decided to try, with God's
help and the assistance of all who were willing to
engage in the good work, to do what we could in the
interest of temperance.

PIONEERING IN THE SAN JUAN

To do this work in a "live" mining-camp, where so many were engaged in the devil's own business, needed wisdom as well as courage, that the work might be pushed vigorously without creating a feeling of hatred toward those who favored temperance.

When first mentioned I met opposition where I least expected it—from Christian men, officers in the church. Not that they opposed temperance work, but saloons, gambling-halls and dance-houses were so numerous that it was considered unwise to attempt reform work.

Having but one motto—the same I afterwards placed at the head of my religious newspaper, "If God be for us, who can be against us?"—I said to the church officers: "If I cannot deliver my lectures in the church I will deliver them some other place." No objections were made to my using the church building.

The first lecture was given December 18, 1877,—subject: "Come, Take a Drink." That all might know what to expect, I had posters printed with "Come, Take a Drink" in large letters, and the rest of the poster in small type. The posters were placed everywhere, not forgetting to put a liberal supply in the saloons. The subject struck the saloon-men's "funny bump," ànd all made some good-natured remark about "being on hand that night to take a drink with the Parson."

Every night while the meetings were held our church was packed, men standing in the broad aisle, and all the vim and vinegar the Parson possessed were put into those lectures.

By referring to my Pastor's Register I find written, "Grand success! God with us in the movement! Eighty-four signed the pledge the first night!" The good work went on for thirty-one nights. Over six hundred signed the pledge. Night after night men came forward and signed who had the manhood to keep the pledge. Among the number was one who is now an honored minister of the Gospel, doing a grand work for the Master. At the time I believed him to be an unpolished diamond; and it has been so proven, for a more successful worker cannot be found.

At first the "whisky element" laughed at the idea of much being done in the line of temperance work in a "live" camp. Being without knowledge either of the love or the power of God, they supposed that they would remain undisturbed in their wickedness. But before the meetings progressed one week the "whisky element" had organized to fight the movement, and a few Christians were timid

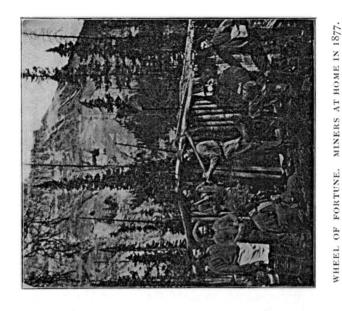

WHEEL OF FORTUNE.   MINERS AT HOME IN 1877.

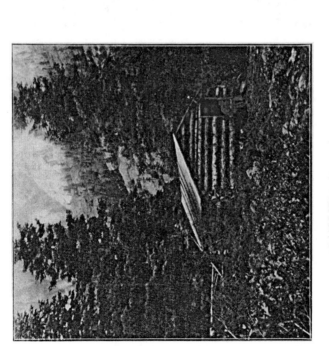

PROSPECTOR AT HOME.

enough to ask their pastor to be "cautious" in all he said; for some of the lectures had "created a great deal of feeling." But the pastor did not have a "cautious fit on" and, knowing that he was right, went ahead.

After lecturing on the subject, "Does It Pay?" I could see by the looks on the faces of my best friends that they thought I had said too much. Not having said anything I was unwilling to "back," I stepped from behind the pulpit and remarked: "I have one request to make of my friends, and that is, not to offer apologies for anything Mr. Darley has said, for I mean every word, and am ready to face any man who objects without a pulpit between us; for this is a square-toed fight between right and wrong." A saloon-keeper standing near the door said: "Damn him, let him go; the more we say, the worse he gets."

Before the meetings closed almost all the attorneys in camp had made one or more temperance speeches. The Catholic priest delivered one temperance lecture for us. All "old timers" remember those meetings, and since leaving San Juan I have met men who then signed the pledge and have kept it.

While the movement was at its height I met four

men, on Silver Street, all decked out in blue ribbons
—ribbon around their hats, around their waists and
from their shoulders to their waists—all as "drunk
as lords!"—all had signed the pledge! So soon as
they saw me, they began yelling: "Here are some
of your converts, Brother Darley!" I thought that
they looked as though someone had converted them,
but surely the Lord had not.

One night during Christmas week, after a very
interesting and successful meeting, Mrs. Darley
said: "My heart aches for the young men in this
camp, away from home and home influences. I
wish our house were large enough to keep open
house on New Year's Day; we could then invite
every young man in the camp to call." After consultation we decided to try to rent a large store-
building that was vacant, if it could be secured, and
then ask the ladies to meet and consider plans.
Early next morning we learned that we could have
the building free. With the same energy and pluck
that had characterized their former work, the ladies
began making arrangements. It was announced
that they would keep open house in said store-building, on New Year's Day, from 9 a. m. to 10 p. m.
Long tables were set and loaded with substantial
food; a piano was provided and the day enlivened

with music; in the evening brief addresses were made. The pledge was placed on a table near the door and forty-five signed it.

Only two intoxicated men were seen in the camp New Year's Day. Toward evening I met one of them, a young man, and after talking to him invited him to go home with me. We talked for over an hour. When leaving my house he said: "I will not promise to sign the pledge, but will walk around till I am sober; then I will go to the store-building."

About 9 p. m. he came in, ate a hearty meal, and without being asked signed the pledge. Years afterward I met him in Alamosa. He told me he kept the pledge six months. Our ladies received over six hundred calls. This was the way we kept open house the first day of the New Year, 1878, in a "live" mining-camp.

CHAPTER VIII

"BURRO—PUNCHING"

"All things hold their march
As if by one great will;
Moves one moves all—
Hark to the footfall
On, on forever."   —*Miss Martineau.*

"Burro-punching" is a familiar term, where the business is followed, and means to walk behind a "pack-train" punching the patient, sure-footed and valuable, although greatly abused little animal.

Often have I walked behind a burro when going to preach the Gospel in the "regions beyond." The term "burro-puncher" became so common during the early days of the "Great San Juan Excitement" that all who had anything to do with the little animal were called "burro-punchers." Some who are now counted among the "leading lights" in Colorado were glad to have a burro carry their "grub" and blankets when first they went into the San Juan. This was a safe way of traveling, considering the roughness of the trails. No one feared being wrecked by a misplaced switch or a broken rail. Having our own provisions and blankets, we were independent travelers.

As a personal and particular friend of the faithful beast that has done so much to help develop Colorado, I regret that many believe the burro has cultivated the swearer as much as he has the state. Those who abuse the burro and swear at him like a pirate, curse everything; not because they are provoked, but because they are habitual swearers. When men have excused themselves for cursing on the ground that the burro is a "stubborn animal," I have answered: "Treat you as a burro is treated and you will become as stubborn as he."

The general belief among packers seems to be that a burro has no feeling, knows neither joy nor pain and expects to be mistreated. Burros suffer terribly, and if men are to be punished for cruelty to animals (I sincerely hope they may be), some men will discover that none of God's creatures can be tortured and the culprit go free. "A righteous man regardeth the life of his beast," but the average "burro-puncher" seems to think that burros never die. They "just dry up and blow away." I admit they are hard to kill. A "baby burro" fell from the top of a cliff sixty feet in height, into the Gunnison

River, and was not injured. On Bear Creek Trail, about five miles above Ouray, one packed with flour fell two hundred feet; the weight of the flour turned the burro heels up, and, striking in the snow, his life was saved. Yet the animal can be killed and it sometimes dies a natural death. While crossing deep streams, unless their ears are tied, they will drown; but by tying them up they can be pulled across without danger.

After a rope is tied to the burro's neck he is pushed into the stream. The men on the opposite bank begin pulling and, although the burro may go under repeatedly, he is landed all right. As soon as his ears are untied his voice is loosened and breaks forth in trumpet tones of rejoicing, loud enough to be heard far and near.

Those who are unacquainted with the trails in new mining-regions, and the way men travel through Indian countries where there are no houses, bridges or wagon roads, have no idea of the difficulties that must be faced. In the winter of '79 a man brought a burro from Mineral Point, at the head of the Uncompahgre River, over Engineer Mountain, to the head of Henson Creek, on snow-shoes. He made the shoes of sole leather and taught the burro to use them. It was slow work, yet he succeeded in getting his "jack" across the range. This may sound "fishy," but it is true. Where a burro and a "burro-puncher" cannot go, no other creature need try.

CHAPTER IX

"An old divine once wrote from the frontier to the students
of Princeton: 'We want strong oxen here; we have plenty of
roots.' "   —*R. A. McConnell, Esq.*

My first trip into the Animas country was made
at the request of Rev. Sheldon Jackson, D. D., who
was Synodical Missionary for more territory than I
can remember.   At that time the Synod of Colorado
embraced Colorado, Wyoming, Utah, Montana,
New Mexico, Arizona and any other portion that
was "lying around loose."

In company with two gentlemen, one an editor,
afterward a partner with "Brick" Pomeroy in his
big tunnel scheme near Breckenridge, Colorado, I
started for Animas City.   The object of my trip
was to explore the Animas country in the interest
of religion in general and of Presbyterianism in
particular.

All went well until we struck the deep snow on
the range between the Lake Fork of the Gunnison
and the headwaters of the Animas River (above
"timber line").   It was in July, 1877.

PIONEERING IN THE SAN JUAN

A trail had been packed by the "burro-punchers," that they might cross to Animas Forks with their pack-trains. Being very narrow, the editor's horse stepped out of it, and down went the horse. Then the fun began. The more the horse plunged the deeper he went. We were without shovels, and therefore in trouble; but fortunately we found, near timber line, some miners working a "prospect." With their shovels and assistance we managed to dig and pack snow until we got the horse on the trail. At Animas Forks we parted company with the editor and journeyed down the Animas River, reaching Silverton that night. In the morning I asked the man who fed my horse—two feeds of corn of five pounds each—how much I owed him. He said he had often heard of Mr. Darley, and guessed I was the preacher, and would not "strike" me very heavy. My bill was two dollars and fifty cents, or twenty-five cents a pound for the corn. I paid it and thanked the man, for I knew the amount was very reasonable. Corn packed in on burros means expense. One man who had the same amount of corn and hay for his horse, swore like a trooper when he found his bill was five dollars; but his swearing did not reduce the amount for horse feed. The man who furnished the feed remarked, very dryly, "I am not in this country for my health." This swearer wanted to be piloted to Animas City, a town at that time of thirty-three cabins. When we were introduced I could see, by the curl on his lips at the mention of "Reverend," that he would not be an agreeable traveling-companion. Our party increased to four. This swearer was called a gentleman because he had money, wore good clothes and went in polite society.

Many believe that "rough men" or else the smooth sporting characters are the men who delight to swear at and, if the opportunity is given, insult a minister of the Gospel. Nothing could be farther from the truth. Such men, as a general rule, treat a minister respectfully. The class who love to jeer and insult ministers belong to what are commonly called "smart Alexes"—men who claim to have been "well trained," dress well, read infidel books and make pretensions to some position in what they call good society.

I had "sized" my man up and concluded that he had more impudence and general cussedness about him than brains; so was ready for him. The trail was extremely rough. My horse was small and had been on more trips than were for his good. On that part of the trail known as "Old

Coal Bank Hill," when a long way up, my horse fell while jumping to catch a footing, and rolled more than fifty feet. I was walking behind and came near being carried down with him. The trail was certainly rough.

Before going far my swearing acquaintance seemed disposed to enliven the hard ride of almost sixty miles by having some fun at the "Parson's" expense. He finally called out: "Parson, this is not the road to heaven." Being already loaded, I answered: "No, but there are plenty of such men as you on like trails going to hell, and I am doing what I can to save them." That ended his attempts to have fun at the "Parson's" expense.

We failed to reach Animas City that night, so were compelled to camp. I was without blankets, but my companion shared his. It being my object to find out as much as possible about that part of Colorado, I left the party next morning and started for Hermosa Creek. Finding a well-worn deer trail, I followed that. It led me to a portion of the creek which proved to have a bad crossing. The banks were steep and the water deep. My horse got down, and so did I.

That night, tired, wet and hungry, the first Presbyterian minister—and so far as I know the first minister—rode into the little place called Animas City, near where the flourishing town of Durango now stands.

After a night's rest and a warm breakfast I concluded, before visiting the people, to try to find someone who would either shave me or loan me a razor. Among the log cabins was one larger than the others, with the familiar sign over the door, "Saloon." As I drew near that public place of various kinds of business, I asked a man if he knew where I could get shaved. "Yes," said he, "you can get shaved in a little room in the back end of that saloon." I walked in and on through to the little room and, sure enough, there was an intended barber's chair—a box upon a box, with a board nailed to it at about the right slant for a barber's chair. In front of this fix-up was a glass, some bottles, and a few razors. The room was chiefly used for another purpose.

Four men were playing "poker." The room being about eight by ten feet, we were a little crowded for space; but that was the least of my troubles. When I looked at the man who did the shaving I confess that, if the four better-looking men who were gambling had not been in the room, he would not have shaved me. If whisky ever

67

blossomed in full, it was on that man's face. He apologized for his looks by saying that he was "just recovering from a very severe attack of erysipelas." Did it not sound harsh, I should say, from a very severe spell of the "jimjams." His razor was dull and his hand quite unsteady. Finally he finished a twenty-five cent job of scraping. I paid the bill, told the crowd there would be preaching somewhere in town that evening, invited all to come and walked out. That night I preached to a fair-sized audience and secured signers to a petition for a church organization.

By referring to my "Pastor's Register," I see that my text was Ephesians 2: 8; subject, "Grace"; date, July 10, 1877. When I think of that trip as I write this chapter, it seems to me the subject should have been "Grace and Grit."

The next day I bought a beautiful "red-tanned" black-tail deer skin from a Navajo Indian for one dollar. The skin made me a pair of fine leggings.

When I reached home after my first trip into the Animas country, having ridden nearly two hundred miles over as rough trails as ever I saw, I was tired; but home missionaries in those days, who preached on the frontier, had to "tire and tire again."

CHAPTER X

"The whole universe of God will crumble to pieces before God will overlook or despise one single tear of genuine repentance." *—Judge Mc Williams.*

———

"I want to keep alive my head in my heart." *—Doddridge.*

From what has been written regarding mining-camps many have concluded that, in the early days of a "live camp," when the first great rush is made and the excitement over reported "rich strikes" and "strikes" that are "rich" runs high, the majority of men who go to such camps and are carried away by the fever are rough characters. This is not the case. The majority are intelligent, enterprising and plucky; many are cultured, "traveled men," who have seen much of life and are in the habit of doing their own thinking.

Mr. Josiah Copley, after visiting several of the mountain towns in southwestern Colorado, wrote the "Presbyterian Banner": "I have found in those towns much intellectual force and bold iniquity." From this we see the impression made on the mind

of an intelligent man like Mr. Copley, whose home
for more than fifty years had been in Pittsburg, Pa.

True, there are many "hard cases" in our mining-
camps; and while in the San Juan I was often
reminded of what a Dutchman said to one of them:
"You get off from mine house, or you give dis name
a bad blace." In Lake City that class lived near
Henson Creek. This part of the camp was well
named "Hell's Acre," for the first part of the name
was about all that was ever raised on that acre.

There was always a sad thought in my mind connected with this portion of our camp; i. e., that so
many young men who had been well trained in eastern homes would visit the dance-halls to see something of "wild life" in a frontier mining-camp during
its palmy days. One Sabbath night, after preaching,
I went to my little shanty, eight by ten feet on the
outside—one side six feet high, the other eight, with
the fireplace built outside that I might have more
room on the inside; my bed being made of "Colorado
feathers" (shavings),—when, to my astonishment,
I found that the shanty had been broken into. A
shirt, a coat and a valise that had been left in my
care, containing valuable mining papers and family
pictures, had been stolen. I was surprised that any
one would dare to steal in a new mining-camp, for

the culprit, if caught, would most likely receive such punishment that no more would be needed in this world.

The one thing to do was to try to recover the stolen goods, especially what had been left with me for safe-keeping. I first placed in my pocket what a colored pastor rebuked a member of his church for carrying and received the following answer: "Don't the Scriptures say, 'Be ye always ready'?" Then I went to "Larry" Dolan's gambling-hall and found the officer I preferred to help me find the thief. From there we went through the halls of like character; then started for "Hell's Acre." In the first large dance-hall we entered I saw a number of young men dancing who had been in my congregation not more than two hours before. In the last hall we entered a woman known in camp by a name that would hardly sound euphonious, told me that a "carpet bagger" had just left the hall with a coat over his arm and a valise in his hand. As the officer and myself stepped out of the door one of the bar-tenders shot a man in the neck. We failed to find the thief, but the next day the valise and papers were discovered.

Often during those years I was reminded of the truths taught in the seventh chapter of Proverbs:

"Her house is the way to hell, going down to the chambers of death." Many young men from good homes in the East seemed to forget, or at least neglect, the instructions given them when they left the fireside.

A PICTURE

At first, letters were written to loved ones "back home." They were filled with descriptions of what the young man saw and, underneath it all, in lines that were plain, the mother thought that she discovered a desire in her boy to return home, and said: "He is homesick." But months pass, and in our imagination we look into that old home nestling among the eastern hills, for we are anxious to learn what the mother now thinks of her boy. She says that of late he has not written so often as he did at first; his letters are much shorter; he complains of being so busy. The tears of sorrow that very many sons are daily bringing to mothers' eyes are not seen; still the pale, careworn look and the heart-sickening smile that is forced to that worried mother's face, tell plainly the thoughts that are in her mind and the struggle that is going on in her heart; and what is still plainer, her words, not of regret, but of what borders on joy (while speaking of a son she buried ere the flush of manhood mantled his cheeks), tell the sad tale of a wandering boy.

To leave that home and go where we can get a sight of that young man who is breaking his mother's heart; to learn what he is doing, and how he looks, is a task that can be accomplished by visiting any "live" mining-camp. How many young men, and men that are in middle life, drink that which poisons, intoxicates and ruins! They turn their feet toward her house, whose feet the wise man said "take told on hell."

Of the two sorrows that can come to the heart of a mother, the death of a son, or the going away of a son into the paths of sin and folly, the latter is by far the hardest to bear. A profligate son is a much heavier burden than a dead son. One can be buried, and if he has been a true son, his memory will be cherished. But if a son is a living sorrow, oh! how intense the anguish of a mother's heart as she follows him by prayers through the sinks of iniquity! One of the most touching lines I ever read was published in a paper at the request of a heart-broken mother—short, but oh! the depths of love it contained:

"Willie, come home."

May God help the young men who read this book to

live such pure lives that no one will have just cause to feel ashamed of them.

While there is nothing more shocking to behold than the wreck of a dissolute man (unless it be that of a dissolute woman), yet no Christian has a right to shun a prodigal when the wanderer is looking for a kind word or a helping hand. While he is in a deplorable condition, our prayers should ascend for the salvation of the perishing.

> "I saw a vessel which the waves did spare,
> Lie sadly stranded on a sandy beach
> Beyond the tide's kind reach;
> Within its murmur of lamenting speech
> Long lay she there;
> Until at length
> A mighty sea arose in all its strength,
> And launched her lovingly,
> And thus, alas! our race
> Lay stranded on the beach of human sin
> And misery,
> Beyond all help, until God's
> Gracious grace—
> A mighty tide
> All crimson dyed—
> Swept grandly in
> And set us free."

It matters not how high upon the shore the young man's frail bark may have been cast by the waves of temptation; if it be not broken in pieces, it is our duty to try to launch it lovingly once more on the sea of life and, by giving him good advice and a helping hand, induce him to steer his shattered craft by the compass of true manhood, virtue and godliness, bidding him look to God, who "knoweth our frame" and "remembereth that we are dust"; to Him who knoweth the many temptations to which young men are subject.

> "There's a fulness in God's mercy
>   Like the fulness of the sea;
>   There's a kindness in his justice,
>   Which is more than liberty.

> "There's no place where earthly sorrows
>   Are more felt than up in Heaven;
>   There's no place where earthly failings
>   Have such kindly judgment given."

Young men lead fast lives—then write letters home, believing they can convince their parents that they are living aright. But they are mistaken. For Satan writes a legible hand and he writes between the lines of their letters. Young men, remember that each day you are sowing seed that will bear fruit, and, "Whatsoever a man soweth, that shall he also reap."

CHAPTER XI

"The story of human life, with its lights and shadows, its strength and weakness, will be an interesting story so long as the human race shall endure." —*Henry Vincent.*

My "Pastor's Register" reveals a hard roll: "George Elwood, saloon-keeper, killed;" "Luther Ray, murdered in a gambling-hall;" "Charles C. Curtis, killed by a snow-slide while in his cabin;" "Alfred Shepherd, died from exposure in storm;" "Harry Pierce, killed by a premature blast in the Ula mine;" "John Furgerson, killed by a landslide;" and so it reads until I come to "Jackson Gregory and Newton N. Lytle, killed by a snow-slide near the old 'Dolly Varden Trail,' on Engineer Mountain."

To show the spirit that prevailed among men during the early days of the "Great San Juan Excitement," I will describe the way in which they acted. As soon as news reached camp that Jackson Gregory and Newton N. Lytle had been buried in a snow-slide, there was no lack of volunteers who offered to dig them out. Whenever a man volunteered his services for this kind of work he knew

RINGING INTO CAMP THE BODIES OF TWO MEN WHO WERE
KILLED BY A SNOW SLIDE.

RIVER SIDE SNOW TUNNEL, NEAR OURAY, COLO.
450 FT. LONG IN MID-SUMMER.

(This is the celebrated Mears Toll Road. The slide came down in the Winter
and an immense Tunnel, 450 ft. long, large enough for six horse stage, was dug
through it. The snow did not melt all Summer. This is the end of the Tunnel
nearest Ouray.)

what it meant; for in a snow-slide region one avalanche is likely to start another. The proof of this statement was given while the men were working to get the bodies. Shortly after they commenced, a much larger snow-slide, coming from a greater height, was heard thundering and crashing down the mountain-side near the track of the previous one. Every cheek blanched, and every heart beat fast as the slide came with almost lightning speed down from its lofty bed—and had it not struck a spur of the mountain that changed its course, the number of bodies would have increased from two to thirty-two, which the next set of volunteers would have ventured to uncover.

Mr. Gregory was not covered more than eighteen inches; his right arm was above his head, and his face toward the mountain; but having been carried so far, the snow was tightly packed, and death by suffocation must have soon followed. Mr. Lytle was covered by four or five feet of snow; neither body was bruised.

It was a weird and strangely solemn funeral. Both bodies were placed side by side in the little log cabin where Mr. Gregory's family lived, near "timber line." A babe at the mother's breast and seven other children like steps (so near of an age), all gathered around the remains of their father. (Lytle was a bachelor.) Brave men wept as they looked down on the faces of their departed brother miners, and into the face of that widow, and those of her children. You may depend upon it that neither the distance up the mountain side to that cabin home, now desolate, nor the long winter caused those hardy men to forget the needs of the bereaved family.

Having been gone from home two days, and having seen enough to touch a man's heart to its lowest depths, my own home and the loved ones seemed doubly dear. While the men who went to the front as home missionaries, in the early days of church work amid the rugged mountains of Colorado, saw much that touched their hearts and tried their nerves, they also saw things which convinced them that the hearts of true men often beat under a rough exterior. If you want to know a man through and through, put him where he will have to face the music or show the white feather.

It is wonderful how strong the attachments become between men of opposite tastes, different habits and education—differing as widely as is conceivable—when their danger is one, and all realize, and face it like men.

78

CHAPTER XII

"There is a peculiar beauty about godly old age—the beauty of holiness." — *Alexander Smith.*

While calling to mind past experiences, when dangers have gathered around us, we sometimes wonder how we escaped with our lives. We may say that God's everlasting arms were underneath and around us; yet after all we are convinced that there is a hidden mystery about it. Many could in truth trace their escape from death to the "effectual fervent prayers" of some "righteous man" or woman.

In all my varied experience I never had my heart so touched as it was by the recital (one year after that terrible trip to Silverton with "Gus" Talbot, the mail-carrier) of an old lady concerning her deep anxiety and all-night and all-day prayer for my safety. She was a quiet, unassuming, God-fearing woman, not easily approached, said little to any one and seldom went anywhere except to church.

I was making pastoral calls and had been in her

home but a short time, when tears came to her eyes as, with quivering lips, she asked: "Do you remember the terrible snow-storm that swept over this San Juan country about a year ago?" I replied I had good reasons for remembering it. "So have I," said she. "You know you gave notice in church that you would be absent the next Sabbath; that you were going to Silverton to preach and intended to organize a church. I saw you ride by and knew you expected to go as far as Burrows Park with your horse and then snow-shoe it over the range. You know I was the first white woman in all this region and, having lived several years among these mountains, I can tell by the way the clouds hang round the high peaks when there is going to be one of those terrible storms; and I knew by the way the clouds were gathering that before you reached Silverton the storm would overtake you. I knew your disposition so well, and from what I have often heard about you, I knew you would either get to Silverton or die on the range. So when night came on, and, with the darkness, that terrible storm, I prayed for you all that night and all the next day; for the storm still raged, and I knew you were in it somewhere on the range."

So soon as I could control my feelings sufficiently

to speak without showing what some men call weakness—but I do not, for the man above all men "wept"—I said: "Now I know why I lived through that fearful storm."

The summit of the lofty ranges is where the "Storm King" gathers his strength that he may sweep down the rugged mountain sides; and woe betide the traveler who is caught in his arms when the darkness of night as well as the fury of the storm is doubled! No wonder the trees at timber line are twisted and their limbs bent, while they hug the rocks almost like a living thing.

Every severe storm in which I have been has made a lasting impression on my mind; and when muscular rheumatism gets hold of me, I am convinced that those storms have left a deep and lasting impression on my body. It also reminds me of the fact that frontier work, like other kinds of work, has its price. You do the labor and take your pay. Yet, after all, lives there a minister who, looking back and recalling his struggles and hardships on the frontier in the Master's cause, regrets one hour of suffering, one hardship, one danger, or one dollar given to the work? Verily no! Their only sorrow is that they were not able to do more and give more for Him who gave all and suffered more than tongue can tell, that they might live eternally with Him.

The following is a sample of what I find recorded in my "Pastor's Register," under the head of "Register of Funerals": "Donald Robertson, age thirty-five; residence, Capitol, Colorado; place of burial, Lake City; date of burial, November 24, 1879. Lost on the range at the head of Henson Creek; caught in a storm at night; fell about twenty-five feet; froze to death." What intense mental suffering that man endured! What longings for the morning dawn! What weary wanderings hour after hour! Only those who have been on the summit of some lofty range of mountains in a storm at night will ever know.

Like the grand old ocean, when a calm is on her face, she looks so harmless, so quiet—yea, restful—so do our grand old mountains look beautiful, bold and harmless. But when the "Storm King" strikes them, their faces change and they are the opposite of restful. They fill the hearts of men with terror.

CHAPTER XIII

"Many a splendid genius was the despair of a good father when young. But all of a sudden he awoke and went into action like a soldier into battle, and made a name that will live forever."   —*Rev. Day K. Lee.*

Next to the boy who teased the bald-headed man until he gave him twenty-five cents to keep still, and then called it his "bald-headed quarter," Lake City could boast of having the hardest. He was about seven years old. A man who kept a saloon at the "upper crossing" of the old "Slumgullion" stage road, on the Lake Fork of the Gunnison River, died, and I was asked to officiate at his funeral.

The procession was rather short for a mining-camp. If the religion of a certain class of miners ever shows itself, it is at funerals; not, however, for the same reason given by a stingy man—that "the sermon be just as solemn and there is no collection taken"—but to show sympathy.

There were only two wagons—one with the coffin, the widow and driver (the pall-bearers walked); the other a light spring wagon with a driver and the preacher. When passing through camp this irrepressible boy decided to join the procession. After walking a short distance he asked to ride.

All went well until we arrived at the cemetery. A miscalculation had been made as to the time required to do the work of digging the grave. On account of the stones more time was lost than the grave-digger had made allowance for. When we reached the cemetery the grave was about half dug. While talking to the widow the irrepressible boy stepped up to me and asked: "When are you going to put that man in the hole?" Knowing the perseverance of the boy, I invited him to take a walk around the place to see where a "washee man" was buried. At the Chinaman's grave the boy pulled his hand out of mine and left me. Soon he began throwing pieces of dirt at the men who were at work. A man who had walked to the cemetery (not a pall-bearer) slapped the boy, which caused considerable excitement, for one of the pall-bearers, a friend of the boy's father, proposed to "take it up."

When I returned to the little group at the grave the boy was crying bitterly. He being the cause of the trouble, I took hold of his hand, and said: "Come with me"; then he yelled, "Say, when are you going to put that man in the hole?" The little rascal was determined to see that man "put in the hole."

WHO'S NEXT ?

It was evident that some of the men in our camp were determined to be bad; others were reckless while seeking the gold that perisheth with the using, yet all seemed sympathetic. I never saw the time when it was difficult to get pall-bearers for "one of the boys" in a "live" mining-camp. It was considered a post of honor. But realizing as I did that unless a higher value was placed on human life some of the "gangs" living in our camp would soon be "gone over the range" for the last time, I made up my mind that if there was any scare in the "boys" I would bring it out. Being asked to preach a funeral sermon (no ten-minute talk would satisfy that crowd), I was forcibly reminded of the fact that one "gang" would soon need a new set of pall-bearers. By referring to my "Pastor's Register," I saw this was the fourth out of the six original stand-bys for that crowd. The one just killed was particularly well-liked by his associates, and a young man in whom I had been greatly interested.

When about the middle of my sermon, after giving dates of the death of each, and showing that

85

they were unpleasantly near together, and having mentioned the fact that but two of the original six were left, I stopped for a moment, stepped toward the pall-bearers, and shouted, "Who's next?" Afterwards one of the men said, "It made me think for a while, for it startled me."

CHAPTER XIV

GOOD IMPRESSIONS MADE BY WALKING THROUGH DEEP SNOW

"A Christian is like a locomotive. A fire must be kindled in the heart of the thing before it will go."

—M. W. Jacobus, D. D.

Before a minister can be made instrumental in reaching godless men they must first be convinced that he is in earnest, not only in what he says, but in all he does. All men place a value on earnestness; the majority consider eloquence, unaccompanied by sincerity, below par.

For several months I had been preaching every Sabbath afternoon at one of the great mines four miles from camp. One Sabbath morning warm friends and careful officers said: "Mr. Darley, we hope you won't walk to the mine to-day." Over eighteen inches of snow had fallen, and the wind was blowing. I replied: "I must not miss my appointment." After a hearty dinner I changed my pulpit suit for one adapted to mountain trips and put on boots to match.

It took nearly three hours to walk to the mine.

PIONEERING IN THE SAN JUAN

The road was up grade all the way and in many places the snow was waist-deep. Only one man was in the large room where services were held. He looked surprised, and said: "We did not expect you to-day." He started to the "bunk houses," and soon the men came wallowing through the snow. Although tired, it was a treat for me to see the earnest look of inquiry on those stern, weather-beaten, manly faces.

Afterwards the superintendent told me my walking to the mine that Sabbath did great good. The men said: "That preacher must be in earnest, or he would not have walked up here after such a storm."

Rev. Charles Simeon kept the picture of Henry Martyn in his study. Move where he would through the apartment, it seemed to keep its eyes upon him and ever say to him: "Be earnest, be earnest, don't trifle." The great Simeon would gently bow to the picture and, with a smile, reply: "Yes, I will be earnest, I will, I will be in earnest, I will not trifle, for souls are perishing and Jesus is to be glorified." Oh, Christian! look away to Martyn's Master, to Simeon's Savior, to the Omniscient One, and be in earnest.

Earnest men may make mistakes by being a little too enthusiastic; but their good work will far more than overbalance their mistakes. While the man lacking in earnestness may be cautious, he will come as near being useless as it is possible for a human being to be.

DR. DARLEY CARRYING THE GOSPEL TO THE REGIONS BEYOND.

CHAPTER XV

ROUGH EXPERIENCE OF A MISSIONARY'S WIFE AND CHILDREN

"His warm but simple home, where he enjoys with her who shares his pleasure and his heart, sweet converse."—*Cowper*.

"When Mr. Disraeli retired from the Premiership, he was offered a place among the hereditary aristocracy with the title of Earl. He declined it with the intimation that, if there was any reward thought to be deserved, he wished it to be conferred upon his wife, to whom he attributed all his success."

The snow fell to an unusual depth all through the San Juan country early in the fall of 1879. All who were unable to cross the range and spend the winter in "God's Country," or the "United States," as the outside world was called, knew that the fall, winter and spring months would drag heavily; but having made up our minds to face the difficulty, every one seemed hopeful, and all were determined to make the best of our surroundings and enjoy life to the fullest. Those who danced, danced to their heart's content. Those who were especially fond of playing cards whiled away many long hours at the card table; while others enjoyed themselves coasting and snow-shoeing. When Sabbath came the majority went to church. The greater part of the winter we did without luxuries, and at times the things necessary to be reasonably comfortable were scarce; yet no one suffered. While pastor of "The First Avenue Presbyterian Church," in Denver, Mr. Spaulding, who kept a store in the camp in '79, told me that in the winter he sold every pound of apples or fruit of any kind he could get at sixty cents a pound. Everything else that was eatable brought a high price.

Mrs. Darley thought it would be wise, if it became possible, to get out of the camp with the children— two boys, one eight years of age, the other seven, and a daughter one year old. When March came it was considered safe to go with a sleigh by what was known as the "Indian Creek and Cochetopa Pass route." The distance to the end of the railroad was greater than that of the other stage routes, but it was the only way to get out of the San Juan, the other routes being impassable. We knew that something like one hundred and seventy-five miles through the heart of the Rocky Mountains, the greater part of the distance in an open sleigh, at that season of the year, was not a pleasant undertaking for a woman with three young children, especially when the snow was deep on the ranges.

But the pioneers of the San Juan took chances

and traveled when and where they would not now care to travel in an open sleigh. After several consultations with the stage agent and drivers, it was decided that if the prospects for clear weather continued the attempt would be made to get out. The morning Mrs. Darley and the children started was clear, but cold. All went well during the day and the different stations were made on time. At one of them a man was taken aboard who had a flask of whisky with which to keep warm. The driver drank a little now and then. In the evening both of them were feeling jolly. As night came on the party began the ascent of the pass. The snow was deep and in places the road was dangerous. The horses, however, were used to the route and kept their feet, though in portions of the road there was much ice. Mrs. Darley felt that the best thing to do was to keep the children well wrapped in robes and blankets. About the hour of midnight the top of the pass was reached and, by this time, the driver and the man in the boot with him were sound asleep. The horses were keeping the road themselves without any assistance from the driver. Finally a sidling place was reached, and being icy the horses selected the best of the road and allowed the sleigh to run to one side. The result was an upset, at which the horses ran away. All the party had been thrown down the mountain side. The driver had his right foot badly cut, but started after the horses. Mrs. Darley, mother-like, had clasped her babe in her arms still closer when thrown. Unfortunately, she struck her face and left shoulder against a projecting rock, cutting her face in several places, causing the blood to flow freely, and severely bruising her left shoulder. Soon she discovered that she was the only one injured. But the younger boy was nowhere to be found, and the thought came that he was still in the bottom of the sleigh. He was found, however, sound asleep on the mountain side, rolled up in a lot of blankets. The disturbance had not bothered him in the least. The man who was with the driver being too drunk to render any help, the boys began digging in the snow with their hands and feet near some scrub pines (it being at timber line), hoping to find some dry branches with which to make a fire. They succeeded in getting a few, but the man with them was unable to produce a match. The situation was serious. The snow was too deep for walking, and the nearest station was three miles away. The party would have suffered greatly had it not been for soldiers of the regular army. They had a post about one mile from the summit of the pass. As the horses ran by it a guard saw them and awoke the captain in command, who, with a number of soldiers, started to see what was the trouble. Soon they saw baby clothes in the snow, which caused them to quicken their steps. The trunk had been carried some distance by the horses before they broke away from the sleigh. Finally the soldiers found Mrs. Darley and the children and offered to take them to a place of shelter. One of the soldiers took the babe in his arms and started. Mrs. Darley discovered that some of the troops were colored men, and asked who they were, and where they were taking her and the children. Then the captain raised the lantern he was carrying and showed his shoulder straps, at the same time remarking that he was an officer in the regular army. Mrs. Darley knew that she and the children were safe with United States troops. When camp was reached they washed the blood from Mrs. Darley's face and did all they could to make her and the children comfortable. Mrs. Darley thinks the name of the captain was Allen. The next day the party were taken to Saguache, and the evening of the following day reached Del Norte on the Rio Grande River; then staged it thirty miles to Alamosa, the terminus of the Denver & Rio Grande Railroad.

CHAPTER XVI

MOUNTAIN—CLIMBING

"One of the inhabitants of the rock-bound and sea-girt isle of St. Kilda, visiting the outside world, was asked if he had ever heard of God in St. Kilda. "Oh!" was the reply; "you in your fertile home may forget God; but a St. Kilda man never can. Elevated on his rock, suspended over a precipice, tossed on the wild ocean, he never can forget his God; he hangs continually on his arm." *—Selected.*

The following poem was written by Rev. Philip Bevan, D. D., after hearing of the hard trip made across Engineer Mountain in 1877 by Rev. Sheldon Jackson, D. D., and the author of this book. While at the General Assembly, in 1897, Dr. Jackson told me he would write this trip up and have it illustrated:

"Stranger:
    'Up the rugged hills ascending,
    Whither are those pilgrims wending?
    Through the horrid gulches steering,
    In the caverns disappearing,
    Farther, higher, still they climb—
    Will they scale that peak sublime?
    Hurrying 'mid the waste of snows,
    Will they court unbidden woes?
    Would they mark the sun arise

PIONEERING IN THE SAN JUAN

Beaming through unclouded skies?
Surely these some vow would pay
Reverent to the orb of day,
Or they trace the eagle's flight
As he sweeps from height to height.
Ah, they fall! they downward glide,
On the avalanche they ride,
By the icy monster borne
Through the rocks and forests torn.
Prostrate in the canyon deep
Are they buried?   Do they sleep?
Craving gold with latest breath,
Have they found, but grasped in death?
No! they rise and shout aloud,
Answering through the snowy cloud.'

"Herald:
'Stranger!   Not with lust of gold
Have we scaled these ranges bold;
Not to rob the eagle's nest
Have we crossed yon snowy crest;
Not to hail the glowing sun
We the icy peaks have won;
Not to delve in glittering ore
We this wilderness explore,
Not to gain earth's wealth, but show
Richer mines than mortal know.
Higher than the eagle's height,
Teach we man a heavenward flight;
Bring the lamp of life divine

MOUNTAIN–CLIMBING

O'er his darkened soul to shine;
Teach his tongue to pay his vows
Anthemed in God's holy house;
Make the rugged waste afford
Praise and gladness to our Lord;
While each sheltered vale shall rise
Like a blooming paradise.' "

CHAPTER XVII

COMICAL SCENES IN CHURCH

"Men are usually tempted by the devil, but an idle man positively tempts the devil." —*Spanish Proverb*.

We had one lazy citizen, who lived near "Hell's Acre," whom I did not love; but after he fell and broke his neck then I wished I had loved his soul and done my full duty toward reclaiming him. He owned what he called an "express wagon"—others called it by various names; the horse and harness looked as much like that for which they were intended as did the wagon—and with this "outfit" he did hauling. A member of our choir employed said expressman to haul him a load of sawdust. The sawdust was to have been hauled on Saturday (at least, so said the man in the choir); but the expressman did not so understand. He sent his boy into the church for the purpose of asking Mr. Payton "where he wanted that sawdust put." I was reading the Scriptures when I heard an unusual noise; looking up, I saw the boy coming down the aisle. What a sight! Man's boots on, clothes that fitted him like the darky's shirt—"did not touch him anywhere''—hair on end, and as dirty as boys generally get. When near the pulpit he yelled at me as though I were deaf: "Say! is Payton in here?" I turned my eyes toward "choir corner," and the boy's eyes soon rested on the man who had ordered the sawdust. Then he cried: "Say, Payton! father wants to know where you want that sawdust put." I kept on reading, but the urchin was the center of attraction. Elder D. A. McConnell, who sat near the boy, touched his arm and said: "Keep still, you are in church." The urchin answered, "Hey?" The boy's supreme innocence was more than the congregation could stand; his reply caused the pastor and people to lose their dignity for a moment.

We had some of the most dignified men in that church I have ever known; men whose sense of propriety was very keen. Anything savoring of impropriety was frowned upon, particularly by an officer from New Jersey. His whole life was precise, and with his preciseness was mingled a kindly charity for others and a generosity that was refreshing. But terrier dogs and tomcats have but little dignity, and occasionally just as little sense of what is proper in the sanctuary. On a Sabbath evening one of each kind visited the church and, for some unaccountable reason, both walked into "choir corner." Very soon the truth of those familiar words, " 'Tis dogs' delight to bark and bite," were forcibly brought to mind, for the terrier dog and the tomcat were soon at it. Such a racket was never before heard in "choir corner." Down the aisle came a faithful elder and our proper New Jersey man after the combatants. Both men quickly realized that they had a job on their hands, but, being Presbyterians and believing in the perseverance of the saints, they captured dog and cat; yet not until services had been suspended. It was amusing to see the dignified way in which our proper man carried that cat and what a determined walk the elder had. The cat was held by the nape of the neck, the dog in arms. I was told that the cat was thrown across the street. Thus ended the row in "choir corner." Since then I have often wished that all rows in "choir corner" might be ended in as short order, if not in the same way. Choirs are a great blessing when they are what they ought to be—a help in every good work; but if they become what they were never intended to be—a cause of disturbance in the church—then thrice happy is that church where no choir is.

A black-tailed deer in church is something unusual, even in a "live" mining-camp. Men who have had much experience with deer know they are easily tamed and, if permitted, will follow their owners. In the early days of the San Juan excitement deer were plentiful, and still are in portions of the same country, although the "steam horse" has taken the place of the freight-wagon and burro pack train. A man living in camp had shot a doe and captured the fawn belonging to her. He kept the deer until it had grown quite large and let it run about the town. No dog could get the best of it. A big buck deer with great horns is not easily handled. Finally the deer went away and no one knew what had become of it. Many expressed themselves as being pleased that it had gone, for they were afraid of the animal. The deer was inclined to be ugly. One Sabbath evening, after the congregation had gathered and I was sitting behind the pulpit waiting for the ringing of the second bell, this large deer walked into the church and half-way down the aisle, seemingly pleased with the lights and the fright he was giving the ladies. He turned round, walked out, and went back to the hills without waiting for collection or sermon.

CHAPTER XVIII

"It is remarkable with what Christian fortitude and resignation we can bear the sufferings of other folks."—*Dean Swift.*

It is a good thing to look up, and very necessary when crossing a swollen stream.

It matters not how strong a swimmer your horse may be, you must not forget your danger and the folly of looking into the stream. Swiftly running water will make most men dizzy and cause them to fall out of the saddle unless they look up.

In June, '77, in company with H. C. James, M.D., I started from Ouray to cross the Ute Indian Reservation, a distance of one hundred and twenty-five miles. The weather being pleasant and our horses fresh, we thought that by taking the old "Cimarron Cut-off Trail," we could ride through in two days, if we went without blankets or extra load. One night out without blankets would do no hurt; and although cool in the mountains at night we could build a fire and be quite comfortable. Some business matters detained my companion, so we did not leave Ouray until 2 p. m. We hoped to reach the home of the head chief of the Utes that night; failing to travel that distance we would stop with the agent. On reaching Cow Creek, about sundown, we found that we had more than we bargained for. The stream was high and rushing onward with all the strength and fury the melting snows could give it, so broad and deep that it made a river. The doctor had a fine American horse. I had a "bronco"; he was wiry, but light-weight.

We would not go back and we hardly dared go forward; but, having only a lunch in our pockets, we must decide. Finally we resolved to cross the stream. The doctor was an experienced hand at the business, and the preacher had tried it often enough to know that there was nothing particularly pleasing about it. The doctor kept his horse's head turned up stream until the swiftest water was reached and so crossed without great difficulty; but I fared differently owing to the lightness of my horse. He struggled hard, but his head turned down stream and we were swept back to the bank whence we started. After resting, the second attempt was made with like result and the third and fourth were also failures. By this time my horse was tired and the doctor was urging me not to try it again. But being wet, and night coming on, I was determined to risk crossing once more. After another breathing-spell I concluded to try higher up, where the stream was narrower and deeper, hoping to be able to get past the center before the head of the horse would be turned down stream. My hopes were realized. I was truly thankful when safe across. We knew that the Uncompahgre River would be impassable, so did not attempt to reach the agency. We made the best of it for the night and were on the trail by four o'clock next morning.

About noon we came to a branch of the Cimarron River. In crossing the doctor almost lost his life by looking into the water. He was nearly out of the saddle, hanging to the horn and the horse's mane. I saw his danger and called, "Look up!" which he did, and soon reached his place in the saddle.

One who has not been carried down a swift mountain stream can scarcely imagine how the water affects the head. You feel as though you were going at a terrific rate, although your horse may be holding his own to a wonderful degree.

It was but a few miles to the other branch of the Cimarron, which was wider, deeper and swifter. That same month a young man and his mule were drowned while trying to cross this branch. By the time we reached it we were tired and our stomachs were empty. But we must cross, though it was dangerous. We breathed easier when over, and, having let our horses graze for an hour, struck the trail and made Indian Creek that night at ten o'clock. We had ridden some sixty miles since 4 a. m. Next day we arrived at Lake City, glad to get home.

In February, 1890, I rode in a palace car over part of that country and found prosperous towns where, in '77, the Ute Indians and wild animals had full possession. I could hardly realize that such a change had taken place and did not regret that I had preached the first sermon in all the Uncompahgre region.

A Presbyterian minister carried the Gospel to the "regions beyond" in that country and, be it said to the credit of our Board of Home Missions, they showed their appreciation by a generous response to all my requests, as did the Board of Church Erection.

On one hard trip, after crossing the Uncompahgre River, I found the camp of two trappers—"Oregon Bill" and "Happy Jack." The latter was the most dime-novel-dressed trapper I ever met. His entire suit was made of "red tan" buckskin, fringed with enough Indian trappings to suit the blackest-eyed dusky maiden in the Ute tribe.

I carried a small flask of whisky to use in case of an emergency. So, after sitting a while at the camp-fire, I drew said flask and began rubbing my swollen limbs. Both men looked on, and soon "Happy Jack" said: "That is the greatest waste of good whisky I ever saw; why don't you drink the whisky and rub your limbs with the flask?" For four days and three nights my clothes had been soaking wet and part of the time frozen, so that the hospitality of the trappers was appreciated.

CHAPTER XIX

A HOME MISSION PROBLEM

"Henry, if each time you do as well as you can, your efforts will average about right."
—Dr. Lyman Beecher to his son Henry.

Home missionaries who did the hard work on the frontier, before the "steam horse" cut the price on freights—they who were paying ten dollars per hundred for flour, thirteen cents a pound for potatoes, one dollar a pound for butter and seventy-five cents per dozen for eggs—will enjoy the following:

Under "Rule Three" (in the commissions used years ago), for congregations applying for aid to the Board of Home Missions, we read: "Congregations should steadily aim at self-support as soon as possible." Five years are placed as a reasonable time in which to accomplish this.

It reads well and looks plausible. But let us figure on the five-year system as it has worked on a great many mission fields; or probably we should say, as it has tried the missionaries who have occupied them.

First year, a church is organized; name, "First

Presbyterian Church.'' Nine-tenths of its members bring their letters from other denominations. But few of them are deeply interested in the future prosperity of the church. Before the church-building is completed one shows a disposition to pull one way, another another way. Yet dedication day comes. The money to pay the remaining indebtedness is pledged. Soon after an article appears in one of our church papers: ''Church Dedicated Free of Debt''—''Blue Banner of Presbyterianism Foremost in the Fight, Carrying the Gospel to the Regions Beyond.'' Oh, yes! Sounds well. Those who have subscribed are called upon. One says, ''I will pay,'' but does not; another says, ''I thought so and so when I subscribed;'' another leaves for parts unknown.

The missionary has dedicated a church with a debt, which makes him feel very uncomfortable; but since there is a kindly feeling existing between the people and himself, he says: ''No reason to feel discouraged.'' With zeal for the Lord's cause, and ''If God be for us, who can be against us?'' for his motto, he goes to work manfully, with a firm determination not to growl, but to right things. Application is made to the Home Board for assistance; but the Board is unable to grant what is asked. The members of his church are unable to keep their part of the contract. The missionary, or else his wife, has a little money on hand and decides to use it rather than leave the field, saying: "All will be well in the end; prospect is good; pull through this year, and all will be lovely." He pulls through; feels happy, sends in an encouraging report to the Home Board, and asks for less the second year than he did the first.

Possibly the Home Board takes it for granted that, since the missionary managed to survive last year on less than Presbytery voted him, he can do so again. His commission is made out for less than is asked, and for less than is necessary to live. He receives his commission and, with a heavy heart, takes his troubles "to the Lord in prayer"; then gets out his expense book. The missionary and his wife figure a while, talk matters over and conclude that the Lord will provide. The next morning the missionary calls on his grocer and tries his level best to convince him that everything will be all right in time.

With a little cough and a kindly smile, the gentleman at the store expresses his sincere desire to see the church prosper—but, ah!—yes—just so. Probably some other missionary has gone home saying:

"The faith of man is very weak." To make a long story short, he begins trading at another place and, when he reads, "Owe no man anything," wonders if that refers to the man who is "carrying the Gospel to the regions beyond."

The missionary tries to keep cheerful and chooses for his text Sabbath morning: "I have learned, in whatsoever state I am, therewith to be content." He preaches his sermon with all the earnestness with which his debts have inspired him. At the close of the service some good brother takes him by the hand, saying: "How your sermon comforted me!" And, as a matter of course, the preacher adds a few more words of comfort. Yet, in spite of his determination to be brave, he becomes pale and nervous. Some sympathizing friend remarks: "You are overworking yourself; if I were you I would take a trip to ———," naming some place that would take more money to reach than the missionary would accumulate in a year, should he live on scenery and light air during that time and save his salary for the trip.

But since every cloud has its "silver lining," and the darkest day is supposed to have an end, the missionary plucks up courage and is purposed never to say die. He says: "My debts are many and badly scattered; this is distressing. How can I remedy the evil?" After consulting his wife—that great blessing to missionaries, for a greater help than a faithful, uncomplaining wife cannot be found—he decides to owe but one man. The banker will in all probability loan the money at two per cent a month (that was the lowest rate of interest in the San Juan; I have paid twice as much). He borrows the money and comes within one of owing no man anything. He is in better spirits; the dark clouds appear to be passing away; his year is nearly out and everyone says the prospects for the future are good. A church meeting is called. The missionary, true to his trust, tells the people that it is their duty to do all they can to make the church self-supporting. He says: "The Home Board is in debt. Let us try to raise more money this year than we did last."

More is pledged (some of the subscriptions would be considered by those who take nothing but "gilt-edged" paper for security as rather scaly). The application for aid is made, sent to the Presbytery, voted on, goes to the Home Board—and lo! the same shearing process takes place again; not from any lack of sympathy on the part of the Board, but from necessity, because the church at large fails to furnish the money required to pay living salaries to her missionaries. Commission comes to the missionary for less than he expects; the ghost of a note is due at the bank; a kindly, gentlemanly Christian request comes from the superintendent of missions to take up another outpost and carry the work forward. All, like an armed force, meet the home missionary; and in blank despair he says: "What shall I do?"

If some good soul, who has the time, will please figure how a missionary, under these circumstances, can make a church, where his congregation is continually changing, self-supporting in five years, he will greatly oblige many home missionaries. The process looks to me a good deal like Paddy's experience with his horse—"one straw less each day," but when the horse got down to one straw a day it died.

CHAPTER XX

"God has put something noble and good into every heart which his hand has created." *—Mark Twain.*

There is a vast difference between the miner and the prospector. Many think these names synonymous, but they are not. They represent two distinct classes of men, whose dispositions and lives are as varied as it is possible to imagine. A miner is one who works in the mines, has a home and labors for wages. You are liable to find him in the same place month after month. The prospector is one who will not work in a mine any longer than it takes to earn a "grub stake," or else he gets some one to "stake" him. He seldom has a home, but he does possess a burro, a prospector's pick and shovel, some cooking utensils for camp-life, a few blankets and hope and faith enough to supply an ordinary church—if it were only hope and faith in heavenly things.

Had I the ability to paint a picture of these two graces it would be altogether different from anything I have ever seen painted to represent them.

PIONEERING IN THE SAN JUAN

The picture would be the prospector starting out with his burro packed, headed for some "new find." Job said: "Surely there is a vein for the silver, and a place for the gold where they fine it." A prospector once corrected me on this passage of Scripture by arguing that the word "fine" should be "find." A prospector always hopes to find the "hidden treasure." He talks of it by day and dreams of it by night; the one all-absorbing question that possesses his mind is: "Where can I strike it rich?"

In the seventies there was not much finery nor a great attempt at show in dress throughout the San Juan; but there was enough sympathy, good will, kind deeds and big-hearted hospitality to fill a state and bless the human race. During these years the few ministers who went to the front found no palace cars in which to ride and seldom a horse to mount. Walking was reasonably good and fashionable. Miner, prospector, merchant and preacher were privileged to walk.

Often while preaching in the camps where the men were mostly prospectors, I have said: "Friends, while you are trying to 'strike it rich' on earth, remember that there is a richer 'lode' in heaven than can be found here. All who 'prospect' for

PROSPECTOR ON HIS WAY TO A NEW GOLD FIELD.

PROSPECTOR RETURNING "BUSTED."

it, find it; and in addition to finding the 'lode' they have great joy in their hearts; and while that realized now will not build you a fine mansion here, all who find shall at last see that they have built a mansion in heaven so grand and fair that the mansions of earth sink into insignificance when compared to it.

"Sinner, whether you are a mining sinner or a prospecting sinner, do you wish to be 'staked in' on this 'lode,' and have your name recorded in the Book that our Creator keeps, in which are written the names of all who are interested in it? If so, go to Christ; tell him you have thus far sought the gold and silver that perisheth with the using—the 'veins' of silver and gold—but now you desire an interest in the imperishable riches, and in the fine gold of God's mercy, love and goodness; and, above all, an interest in the atoning blood of Christ.

"Will you do this? Will you mine deep in the love of God or will you be satisfied with what the earth offers, and reject what is offered you by a loving Savior—'the pearl of great price,' 'the one thing needful'?"

Then, as now, it was but one step from the serious to the ridiculous. I remember meeting a prospector, with whom I was well acquainted, just after he had "made a sale." The amount he had received was not large, but to a man who had been "rustling for a grub stake" for four or five years it was good. Having congratulated him on his success, I said: "I hope you are not forgetting the one thing needful." "One thing needful?" said he slowly, then asked: "What's that, grub?"

CHAPTER XXI

"With malice toward none, with charity for all, with firm-
ness in the right, as God gives us to see the right, let us strive
to finish the work we have begun." *—Lincoln.*

"Were you the man who left a pair of buckskin
leggings at my cabin on the old Uncompahgre trail
about twelve years ago?" was the question asked by
a miner after I had preached the dedicatory sermon
of the new Presbyterian church at Ouray, on the 23d
of February, 1890. I replied that I left a pair of
buckskin leggings, "red tan," in some cabin on that
trail the last trip I made over the range from Ouray
to Lake City. He replied: "It was in my cabin
that you left them." Some one standing by asked:
"Have you the leggings now?"

This conversation was short, but it reminded me of
a hard trip. Friends had begged me not to attempt
to cross Engineer Mountain that day—at least not
without snow-shoes. It was snowing hard in Ouray,
and all knew that at an altitude of more than thirteen thousand feet above sea-level the snow would
be several feet deep. When the "Storm King"

awoke he always made it lively for anyone who tried to visit him in his home on the high ranges or to pass his door. A man looking back over the past can see where he made mistakes. By the time I had walked eight miles up the trail toward the summit of the range, and had reached an altitude of ten thousand feet, it was past noon (had started at 5 a. m.). Coming to a lone cabin, and seeing smoke arising from what was intended for a chimney, I went to the place of entrance and was invited in. Being hungry, after walking through snow that was almost waist-deep—for the storm kept increasing, and the higher I climbed the deeper became the snow—I entered the cabin and gratefully accepted an invitation to "have something to eat." My leggings were wet, so I untied them and placed them before the fireplace to dry.

Dinner over, I started away rather hurriedly, because I was aware that the rest of the trip, or at least to "Rose's Cabin"—below timber line on the Lake City side of the range—would be a hard one, and that no time was to be lost; for if overtaken by night and the range not crossed, it would be terrible.

As I stepped into the snow at the cabin door I went in so deep at the first step that I did not miss my leggings. Nor did I notice that they were gone

THE FAMOUS ROSE'S CABIN ON ROAD TO SUMMIT
OF UNCOMPAHGRE RANGE.

FOUR UTE CHIEFS, AGENT AND INTERPRETER.

until my legs began to grow cold; then I was too far away to turn back. In that cabin I left one of the best pair of buckskin leggings ever owned by red or white man in the old Rockies.

The wind had increased. The snow was so much deeper above timber line, that all I could do was to push my way through. A man almost up to his arm-pits in snow, climbing up the side of a mountain with the snow clouds enveloping him, doesn't do much walking; it is more push than walk. At times it seemed as though I would never reach the top. I could see but a very short distance and that only by holding my hands to my face. Yet I knew the thing to do was to climb. By pushing ahead without getting excited, and by frequent rests, the summit was gained just as the darkness of night began to add to the darkness of the snow-clouds that hung even lower than timber line.

The storm came from the Uncompahgre side of the range; therefore I was able to make my way down the Henson Creek side of the range quite rapidly. By nine o'clock that night I entered a cabin and received the congratulations of what my wife called "some of Mr. Darley's peculiar friends." At noon the next day I reached home with swollen limbs and without my leggings. But the second church ever built in Colorado, west of the Sierra Madre range of mountains, was completed; and the next spring a minister was engaged to work in the camp. The Presbyterians built the first and second churches, on the Pacific slope, in Colorado.

Mrs. Darley said she had never seen me look so haggard and weary, although the year before I had walked one hundred and twenty-five miles in five days and four nights and had suffered all that one man could suffer in that long walk and severe storm ·while crossing the Indian country to preach the Gospel in the "regions beyond."

That eastern readers may know what it meant to cross high ranges when they were covered with deep snow, I copy the following, sent from Ouray to a Denver paper. The paper is dated February 5, 1891: "News has just reached here from Mount Sneffles of the death of four of the Virginius miners, who perished in a snow-slide. They started out from the mine last evening to help bring in Billy Maher, who had been blown up in his cabin about a mile distant. At a point on the mountain, and at an altitude of about thirteen thousand feet, a heavy load of snow was detached and Tom Byron, S. Phillips, Allen McIntyre and John Sanderlin were hurled down the mountain and buried fifty feet beneath the mass, which packed above their bodies as solid as ice. This occurred about ten o'clock last night and the bodies were not recovered until this afternoon. Men worked all night and day with all their power, but could not reach them sooner."

One evening during the seventies, while sitting at table with a number of invited guests, the conversation turned on what had happened the day before. Two prospectors were carried down a mountain side by a snow-slide and buried from five to ten feet; but immediately another slide followed from a greater height, uncovered the men and rolled them out on top of the snow before they were suffocated. They recovered consciousness and reached a cabin where they were cared for. One of the guests said: "No doubt Mr. Darley calls this special providence." Knowing that it was my opportunity for a short talk on special providence, I took advantage of it.

CHAPTER XXII

"Nature's bulwarks, built by Time,
'Gainst Eternity to stand,
Mountains terribly sublime,
Girt the camp on either hand."
—*Montgomery.*

"Who hath measured the waters in the hollow of his hand, and meted out heaven with the span, and comprehended the dust of the earth in a measure, and weighed the mountains in scales, and the hills in a balance?"　　*—Isaiah 40:12.*

"The scenery is awfully grand and it looks as though the devil reigned over all." These words fell from the lips of one of the wealthiest mine owners in the San Juan country. More than twenty years have passed since they were repeated to me, as I stood on the steps of the office talking to the superintendent of the mine, who said them in a way that showed their repetition had set him to thinking. I was impressed with the awful grandeur of the scenery and the fact that an intelligent man could see no traces of his Maker in the "awfully grand scenery" that was before him.

At that time, and since then, the words of the Psalmist have seemed to me peculiarly strong:

CELEBRATED MEARS TOLL ROAD, PROMONTORY POINT.

GRAND SCENERY

"Whither shall I go from thy spirit? or whither shall I flee from thy presence?

"If I ascend up into heaven, thou art there; if I make my bed in hell, behold, thou art there.

"If I take the wings of the morning, and dwell in the uttermost parts of the sea, even there shall thy hand lead me, and thy right hand shall hold me."

If a man cannot see the footprints of his Creator in those "awfully grand," lofty and imposing mountains, where on Nature's face can he see them? They, like grand old Ocean, speak in thunder-tones, saying: "Thy God reigneth." True, the devil reigns in the hearts of many dwellers among the mountains in Colorado, but he does not reign over all. God is among our mountains, ruling the same as in other regions. Man cannot find a place upon all God's footstool where God does not reign.

To me it is a precious truth that none can hide from God. Nor are his children, while in the path of duty, ever beyond our gracious heavenly Father's outstretched arms. Those arms are ever around and underneath us as we look for Him. The harder the work and the less encouragement His laborers receive from without, the nearer the blessed Savior comes and the sweeter the communion we hold with Him. My own experience has been that the longer the journey, the severer the storm, the less the likelihood of my ever looking again into the faces of the loved ones at home, the closer my Savior seemed to be and the warmer grew my heart, as step by step I worked my way through the deep snow or breasted the mountain stream. If God should lose sight of one of His children for a moment, it will be when His loving heart has changed, His strong arms become weak and His all-seeing eye grown dim.

While there is much "bold infidelity" in the mountain towns of Colorado, there are many more faithful followers of Christ than some men would like to have us believe. When the prophet Elijah said, "I have been very jealous for the Lord God of Hosts, because the Children of Israel have forsaken Thy covenant, thrown down Thine altars, and slain Thy prophets with the sword, and I, even I only, am left, and they seek my life to take it away," God said unto him: "Yet I have left me seven thousand in Israel, all the knees which have not bowed unto Baal, and every mouth which has not kissed him."

Elijah thought the devil must be reigning over Israel, for "I, even I only, am left"; but he was greatly mistaken. Instead of being alone he was one among the thousands in Israel who worshiped the true God. In all this there is a lesson, not only for God's children who are laboring in the hardest fields among the Rocky Mountains, but for God's laborers everywhere. We know not what may be going on in the hearts of those among whom we labor. Men do not always speak out the moment they see the error of their ways. Many are thinking about the interests of their souls and, ere long, may join Christ's army. Fight on, faithful ones, and, if need be, suffer on; for victory will surely be yours; whether you labor in the heart of the Rockies, where the scenery is "awfully grand," or in some other place. "For if God be for us, who can be against us?" "He doeth according to His will in the army of heaven, and among the inhabitants of the earth; and none can stay His hand, or say unto Him, what doest Thou?" Remember, that none will be forgotten or unrecognized by the Master when He comes to render to every man according to his work.

If at any time we become discouraged about our work, let us call to mind that it is God's work in which we are engaged; and although we call it ours, in reality it is His. We are the instruments, therefore He will permit no failure. At seasons He will leave us to ourselves, and, instead of helping, observe, to see if we are doing our duty. It is recorded of a Highland chief of the noble house of McGregor that, when he fell wounded at the battle of Preston Pans, his clan, seeing their chief fall, wavered and gave the enemy an advantage. The old chieftain, beholding the effects of his disaster, raised himself upon his elbow while the blood gushed in streams from his wounds, and cried aloud : "I am not dead, my children, I am looking at you to see you do your duty." These words revived the sinking courage of the brave Highlanders and roused them to put forth their mightiest energies, and they did all that human strength could do to stem and turn the dreadful tide of battle.

And may I not with propriety ask, if the knowledge that their chief was looking at them to see them do their duty nerved those brave men and caused them to press forward in the fight, shall not the knowledge we have that our Commander-in-chief is looking at and commanding us to do our duty nerve us for the conflict?

Surely, as Christians, we have as much for which to contend as any class. But, since it is all for the glory of God and the good of souls, we should not hesitate, but go forward laboring earnestly and faithfully at all times, knowing that God sees and will help. All that we do for him, whether it be among his own dear children or that class who persist in saying that the "devil reigns over all," will be rewarded.

"For I know the thoughts that I think toward you, saith the Lord; thoughts of peace, and not of evil, to give thee an expected end.

"For God is not unrighteous, to forget your work and labor of love."

"Sow beside all waters,
    Where the dew of heaven may fall;
Ye shall reap, if ye be not weary,
    For the Spirit breathes o'er all.

"Sow where the morning breaketh,
    In beauty o'er the land;
And when the evening falleth,
    Withhold not thine hand.

"Sow, though the rock repel thee,
    In its cold and sterile pride;
Some cleft there may be riven,
    Where the little seeds may hide.

"Watch not the clouds above thee;
    Let the whirlwind round thee sweep;
God may the seed-time give thee,
    But another hand may reap.

"Have faith, though ne'er beholding
    The seed burst from its tomb;
Thou knowest not which may perish
    Or what be spared to bloom."

CHAPTER XXIII

TERRIBLE HONESTY IN THE FACE OF DEATH

"Deathbed repentance is burning the candle of life in the service of the devil, then blowing the snuff in the face of heaven." —*Lorenzo Dow.*

It is generally believed that every man fears death. Such was my belief once; it is not now. Men become so hardened, or else so careless, that it will take something besides death to scare them. Possibly they have such command over self that we cannot discover the least sign of fear when they are called to face eternity, with all its dread realities to those who know not the truth as it is in Jesus, neither the power nor the love of God. I have witnessed some queer death-scenes—men waiting as calmly for the dark messenger as they would for a meal, with no preparation to meet him.

I visited a young man who was dying. He knew for months that he could not live, yet so far as known he had made no preparation for the great change. I had often talked with him, and noticed a terrible honesty in all he said. The day he died I was sitting holding his hand and talking to him.

After praying with him, as I rose from kneeling, he looked me squarely in the eyes and said: "Mr. Darley" (with shortening breath),

> "The devil was sick,
>   The devil a monk would be;
> The devil was well,
>   The devil a monk was he."

then pressed my hand, and said, "Good-bye."

Often have I stood by the corpse of one who was well instructed in the truths of Christianity, but who had neglected to heed the parting words of parents and friends. As I have looked down at the pale face and then at the stern yet manly countenances of hundreds of miners, my soul has burned within me when I warned them against the putting off the seeking of the "pearl of great price," against preferring earthly treasures before the unsearchable riches of Christ. Some have fallen by the assassin's hand, others have been swept into eternity by the avalanche, that rushes down the mountain side with the rapidity of lightning and from which the hardy prospector has but little chance of escape; others have been killed by premature blasts. One in particular I shall never forget. Young, strong and manly, he looked at his shattered limbs in terror, but could not believe he would die until two or three hours before his death; then came a wail for the grief it would cause his aged father, who was depending on him for support and was a thousand miles away. Others have been frozen to death. Yet, notwithstanding the many dangers with which men are surrounded, hundreds are as reckless as it is possible for them to be. Step by step they scale the giddy height, seeking for hidden wealth. They seem to ignore the dangers about them; they appear to think only of the "bonanza" they expect to strike.

CHAPTER XXIV

"I bid you look into the lives of all men as it were into a mirror."   —*Trent.*

A man's opinion of the Indian varies somewhat according to his experience with him. During the summer of '77 "Cap" Cline's cabin in Ouray was the favorite resort of the Ute chiefs and other Indians, as was also the cabin of Major Call. I ate with and talked to these red men until I became acquainted with them. Among Ignacio's band of Southern Utes was an Indian named Suckett, who greatly desired to drive the white settlers out of the country. The head chief of the tribe was very friendly to the settlers and told Suckett that the next time he came on the Uncompahgre River for the purpose of trying to make trouble, he would kill him, a thing Ouray never hesitated to do when he thought it necessary. Suckett gave no heed to the warning, but came back; when Ouray told Osepa to kill him, which Osepa did. This made the Southern Utes angry, and, it being an Indian's nature to kill someone if a friend has been killed, Ouray sent word to the camp bearing his name for no one to cross the reservation until he told them it would be safe. Col. H. F. Blythe, who was afterwards elected elder of the first church organization in Ouray, and myself, thought there would be no trouble over one dead Indian, so we started with one pack animal and our saddle-horses. Before making our first camp an Indian rode up and began making signs about ponies. We told him we had passed ponies up the Uncompahgre River. He went in the direction in which his ponies were, but in less than ten minutes came back and rode along with us without speaking. As soon as we camped for dinner he sat down and waited until we were ready to eat. We did not invite him to eat, for we needed what provision we had for ourselves; and the Indian was near his own victuals. He came close to what was cooked and sat down, but did not offer to take anything. We emptied a can of peaches on a tin plate, cut some bread and poured our coffee. Colonel Blythe asked if he should pour some coffee in the empty can for the Indian. I knew that, like all the Utes, this one could speak English, and it was nonsense for him to sit like "a bump on a log." I answered: "Not unless he asks for it; and if he reaches for anything we will take a finger off."

EXPERIENCE WITH INDIANS

After we began eating the Indian said: "Coffee." "You can say coffee, can you?" "Yes," said our self-invited guest. A moment later he said: "Sugar." "You can say sugar, can you?" "Yes." Then, "Read." "So you can talk?" "Yes." Then he talked as well as any one; and after eating helped pack, then left us.

We had a delightful trip; the nights were beautiful, and, with our blankets, we kept warm. With the exception of being followed by a party of young "bucks" who demanded "whisky," we had no unpleasant words with the Indians. At one point we found a large crowd watching horse-races. We stopped to enjoy the sport. The Utes have some good horses and understand getting the speed out of them.

At the present day a great deal is said for and as much against the Indian; and most that is said on either side is by those who have studied the question at "long range." In the fall of '60 I first moved to a territory where there were plenty of Indians. Nebraska City was a small place, inhabited principally by the freighters who made it their headquarters. Among them was Alexander Majors, "Pete" and "Gus" Byron and other well-known western men.

PIONEERING IN THE SAN JUAN

The old log fort (old Fort Kearney) was still standing, being used for a jail. I was young, and, having lived until then in St. Louis, Mo., the change was great; everything interested me, especially the Indians. The agent for the Otoes lived in the town, so we saw much of the Indians. One winter several hundred Pawnees camped near us and then we saw more Indians than we cared to see; they were a perfect nuisance. They would walk into our houses without knocking, put their faces against the windows and scare the women almost out of their wits. Occasionally the fingers of an Indian would stick to what did not belong to him. That winter, one who acted as interpreter for the agent of the Otoes, began coasting with us boys. He looked to be about thirty years of age and wanted to be "big Indian." While one of the boys was passing him on the hill (the boy having a faster running sled), the Indian struck him. After the Indian started up the hill the boy said: "If that Indian strikes me again I will knock him down." Another boy said: "You dare not say that to his face." A stone about the size of the boy's hand lay near. He picked it up and started for the top of the hill in company with four other boys.

The Indian was waiting for us. So soon as the

hill-top was reached the boy said: "If you strike me again I will knock you down." The Indian struck the boy in the face; and the boy not only knocked him down, but knocked out his front teeth and cut a terrible gash through both lips, from his nose to his chin. As soon as the Indian came to and got up, he started for the agent's house and came running back with a double-barreled shotgun in his hands. We saw him coming, but the boy who knocked him down refused to run; but he finally "lit out," and reached home in safety. The matter was settled, but it was thought best to keep an eye on the Indian.

Having moved to the San Juan when Colorado was a territory, and having lived near the Ute reservation, crossing it frequently, eating with the Indians and sleeping among them, I know somewhat of their character. I have been with them in Montana, as well as in Nebraska and Colorado. Wherever I went I found them to be as lazy mortals as ever lived.

Yet an Indian has rights that should be respected. To rob him or his tribe of land, whether through misrepresentation or by selling stuff that is useless, or by cutting a double blanket in two and calling it two blankets, is robbery for which no honest man attempts to offer an apology and for which God will call men to account.

Let us not forget that an Indian is a savage and unacquainted with refined, polite and elevated rascality that will rob you in such a way that you are almost compelled to say: "Thank you."

These gentlemanly wolves should not be permitted to deal with the Indian; for savages cannot understand just how it is. All they know is they have been robbed and their only desire is for revenge on some other white man. As a rule it is the innocent man who reaps the revenge of the Indian. Then this outrage is as hard for the whites to understand as the polished way in which the Indian is robbed is for him to understand. Hence our troubles with the Indian.

CHAPTER XXV

A PRESBYTERIAN ELDER'S PLUCK

"A diamond with a flaw in it is better than a perfect pebble."
                                                    —*Selected.*

Sometimes godly men are compelled to do that which seems ungodly to those who have never dealt, worked and associated with rough, boorish and selfish men. Ministers as well as elders have been obliged to use a little "muscular Christianity," that others may understand that ministers, like elders, are only human. Since the elder is a good man to put to the front the minister can remain in the background.

I knew a very devout, intelligent, good-natured elder who had a most surly and irreligious man for a partner. Together they were working a leased mine. They were first-class miners and both were very close run financially. Before signing a contract the elder said: "I want it distinctly understood that I will not work on the Lord's Day, and that will necessitate that we work about one-half day Monday to get the water out that will accumulate in the mine." To this his partner agreed and they

137

began work. The first Sabbath nothing unpleasant was said; but the second (they "bached" in a log cabin) the surly one began growling about "knocking off Sunday" and that it took "a half-day Monday to get the water out of the mine."

The elder made no reply. The third Sabbath, as he was getting ready for church, his partner began swearing at him. This was more than he could stand, and, being a powerful man, he grabbed his partner by the throat and bumped his head against the side of the cabin till he begged for mercy. The elder let him go with the promise to "finish him the next time he dared to swear as he had."

That morning, during church service, the elder looked rather glum, which was so contrary to the man's nature that I knew something was wrong with our good brother. After the close of service he said he wanted to talk with me. He told me what had occurred and added that he ought to have kept his temper; that an elder held a sacred office and his action might injure the church. "What do you think?" I replied: "I think you did just right, and my advice to you is, keep your promise if he ever dares to swear at you again; for you know that I have great faith in 'muscular Christianity,' when properly applied."

A PRESBYTERIAN ELDER'S PLUCK

Such men are worth their weight in gold. Manly, conscientious, kindly, good-natured, yet no one can run over them or the church in which they rule in spiritual things.

ELDER JAMES K. HERRING AND REV. GEO. M. DARLEY, D. D., READY FOR A SWIFT RUN.

CHAPTER XXVI

A BARREL HALF-FULL OF ROTTEN ONIONS FOR A PULPIT

"I don't like these cold, precise, perfect people, who, in order not to speak wrong, never speak at all, and in order not to do wrong, never do anything." —*Beecher.*

I sent word to a saloon-keeper that I would be in his camp on the following Sunday and that I expected to preach in his saloon. On my arrival a man very kindly offered to take care of my horse, so I was at liberty to go where I pleased. When entering the saloon I found that I was to have the use of the room, as requested; but instead of a faro-table, a barrel was placed for a pulpit, with a small box on top which was covered with a white napkin. So soon as I saw that everything was arranged, I was surprised and a little suspicious. Nearing the barrel I discovered what was the matter, and decided to turn the tables on those who had "put up the job" by not seeming to notice that there was anything wrong.

I placed my Bible on the box, and then walked around the room, talking to different ones until time for services.

ROTTEN ONIONS FOR A PULPIT

The text chosen was St. Luke 16: 31—"And he said unto him, if they hear not Moses and the prophets, neither will they be persuaded, though one rose from the dead." The saloon-keeper sat in front of me on a whisky barrel that was laid on its side, so got the full benefit.

When services began he was sitting on the highest part of the barrel. Soon he slid down to one end; then he edged his way up to the middle and then slid down to the other end; thus he put in the time, much to the amusement of those present, and I trust with profit to his soul. Evidently he did not agree with my Calvinistic view of future punishment. I preached for thirty minutes, although almost ready "to quit before I began," and unless those who "put up the job" on the preacher read this, they will never know that the preacher saw the point.

As I was leaving a pleasant-appearing man took my hand and said, "Come again." I felt something soft, and held to it. After taking a few steps I examined what was in my hand and found a twenty-dollar bill. Since then I have preached in large churches without receiving anything more than expressions of appreciation. One peculiarity about drinking men in "live" mining camps is their sense of honor when dealing with a minister; they insist on paying for their preaching and for funeral services.

Often when refusing to accept money for officiating at a funeral, men have said: "Parson, you can't live without money any more than the rest of us." That is so; and if Christians everywhere were of the same opinion the treasury of our Board of Home Missions would never be empty. No doubt ministers are often reminded of the story in which the deacon remarked, after the installation services: "My dear brother, if the Lord will only keep you humble we will keep you poor." A little more generosity would not be a great burden to the Church at large; yet it would be highly appreciated by home missionaries as well as by the boards of our beloved Church.

CHAPTER XXVII

THE KIND OF MEN NEEDED AT THE FRONT

'A great deal of talent is lost to the world for the want of a little courage.''   —*Sydney Smith.*

''The servants of the Lord should be as bold for their Master as the Devil's servants are for theirs.''

—*Countess of Warwick.*

We read about "the relations of higher education to the Christian ministry." The Presbyterian Church papers, in particular, have much to say on this subject; but very little to say on the relations of a higher idea of grace and self-sacrifice to the Christian ministry. Many believe there are fewer inducements for young men to enter the ministry at the present day than there were a half-century ago.

Is there less to draw young men to the ministry now than in the days of the Apostles, or during the first century of the Christian era? Have ministers fewer opportunities to show true heroism now than had those of the Reformation?

There is less inducement along certain lines. We have not so many chances to suffer and, therefore, fewer opportunities of glorying in tribulation. We are not permitted to "take pleasure in infirmities, in reproaches, in necessities, in persecutions and in distresses for Christ's sake," as was Paul. But this should not deter young men from entering the ministry.

The early Christian ministers "were tortured, not accepting deliverance, that they might obtain a better resurrection, and others had trials of cruel mockings and scourgings; yea, moreover, of bonds and imprisonments; they were stoned, they were sawn asunder, they were tempted, were slain with the sword; they wandered about in sheepskins, being destitute, afflicted and tortured, of whom the world was not worthy." The Lord Jesus said of himself: "The foxes have holes, and the birds of the air have nests; but the Son of Man hath not where to lay his head."

What about the sufferings of Polycarp? How did Luther fare in the forests of Germany? What enjoyment had Bunyan in Bedford Jail? What inducements were offered to those who entered the ministry in the dark ages of the Reformation, when the souls of men were tried as by fire? More inducements then than now. Still there are left some for young men of grace, grit, nerve, consecration, energy and intellectual ability.

KIND OF MEN NEEDED IN FRONT

Think of the pleasures such men have when they see the waste places of the "Far West" blossoming and blooming like the rose! Churches built in which to worship our Creator, and sinners brought to a saving knowledge of God in Christ Jesus! There is yet very much to be done before the battle cry of the Church, "Our Land for Christ," is fully answered, as we pray God it soon may be.

On the frontier, among the highest ranges of the Rockies, you can find work that will try all the love for Christ that is in your heart, work, the faithful performance of which will lead you across the track of many a wild and awfully sweeping avalanche, whose roar makes the stoutest heart tremble. Never fear that you will not have opportunities of showing whether or not your religion is the kind that will bear testing. Occasionally the chance will be given of making your bed in the snow; and should darkness overtake you—as it has other missionaries when in a storm—above "timber line," you can spend the night above the clouds.

Young men, say not that the nineteenth century has lost all inducements for you to enter the ministry and endure hardness as good soldiers of Christ. Our land, and especially the Great West, wants men,—brave men, men with Christ in their hearts, men with strong wills, strong faith and an abundance of physical strength. I repeat it, the Great West wants men, brave men, for the enemy's works are strong and the pirate flag of sin has waved already too long in many of our villages and mining camps. Young men, come. Do not doubt but that you will find inducements enough and fields wide enough for usefulness. No matter how talented you may be, all your talents will be needed to make your field bear fruit.

You will find use for your hands as well as for your heart and head, and, when tired and worn and needing rest, even then the cry will be heard:

"Not now, for I have wanderers in the distance,
And thou must call them in with patient love;
Not now, for I have sheep upon the mountains,
And thou must follow them where'er they rove."

Young men, if love for God, for Christ and for souls is not inducement enough for you to enter the ministry, my advice to you is to stay out. If inducements to enter the ministry mean a fine church-building, a wealthy congregation, a pleasant parsonage, a library (such as every minister desires), a session, trustees, superintendent of Sabbath School and everything up to the mark, with a model prayer-meeting thrown in—then I admit that the inducements to enter the ministry are few. But if hard work on fields where souls are perishing for the lack of a faithful minister to point them to the "Lamb of God," and to wield the "sword of the Spirit," as a good soldier, holding it up in all its brightness that it may cut sinners to the heart, putting them into proper shape, making them fit stones for the great temple God is building; or where you may be compelled to labor for months, yea, for years, without gathering one golden sheaf for the Master—then come, if these things mean sufficient reasons for entering the Christian ministry. Get the highest education you are capable of receiving. Then look for a field where you can work and endure hardness, and you will find it.

If you do your duty on some of the fields that are loudly calling for men, you will have the opportunity of feeling very forcibly the words of Christ, when he said he had not where to lay his head; for your pillow will be your saddle, a stone, or the snow.

"When the Batavia was crossing the Atlantic in a terrific storm and there was sighted in the glooming evening twilight a wreck with several men clinging to the shrouds; when it was a question of life or death to man a boat and pull to the rescue, Captain Mouland's call for volunteers . was instantly responded to by twice the number needed for the service. Out of this number he commissioned the picked men, who hastened to their critical trust and, in due time, joyfully returned, bringing in nine rescued souls, amid the hearty cheers of their comrades, who generously envied them the honor of which they themselves had been deprived. When shall the time come that always twice the number of men needed will volunteer for the most advanced and perilous posts of aggressive missionary service, and our only care be to select the strongest and the best? God speed the day!"

CHAPTER XXVIII

"Lapidaries tell us of the Chalcedonian stone, that it will
retain its virtue and luster no longer than it is enclosed in gold.
A fit emblem of the hypocrite, who is only good while he is
enclosed in golden prosperity, safety and felicity."

—*T. Brooks.*

Pray, what kind of Christians are these? The
kind who used to teach in Sabbath Schools "back
East," but who will not teach in Sabbath Schools
"out West." The kind of Christians who used
to "remember the Sabbath Day to keep it holy,"
"back East," but who break it right in two "out
West." The kind of Christians who used to
attend prayer-meetings "back East," but are particular not to let it be known that they are professing Christians while living "out West." They
are the kind of Christians who are walking hand in
hand with the devil, going straight to hell with the
mark of a Christian profession upon them and with
their names enrolled on church books "back East."
They are the kind of Christians who joined some
church "back East," but who never joined the Lord
Jesus Christ. They are numerous "out West." In

the Bible they are called "stumbling-blocks." They
avoid God's house and, by their actions, lead men
to think that they believe the Lord cannot see them
after they cross the Missouri River; and they prefer
that ministers would not bother them until they
recross that muddy stream on their way "back
East," back to where they left their religion. They
belong to that class who never had much to do with
the Lord "back East," but who imagine the Lord
has a great deal to do with them, because he saw
their names on a church book.

Whenever we who live in the West see a professing Christian from the East absenting himself from
church services and the place where prayer is wont
to be made, and persistently and regularly desecrat-
ing the Sabbath Day, going with the multitude to
do evil, we say that man is not a sinner saved by
grace, but a graceless sinner. My heart has often
been made sore by seeing professing Christians
doing many things "out West" that they admit they
would be ashamed to do "back East." Far better
for such persons had they never united with the
church, for now they are "trampling the blood of
the Covenant under their feet as an unholy thing,"
crucifying the Lord of glory "afresh," for which
God will call them to account.

KIND OF CHRISTIANS

"Back-East" Christians, who are living out West without God, let me say to you in all kindness that location does not make the Christian, but the grace of God shed abroad in the heart, and a saving knowledge of God through the Savior. It is the "blood of Jesus Christ, His Son" that cleanses from all sin, and not the placing of your name on a church book "back East." "Not every one that saith unto me, Lord, Lord, shall enter into the kingdom of heaven; but he that doeth the will of my Father which is in heaven."

If the religion of Christ is worth anything "back East," it is worth just as much "out West." And if Christ was in your heart "back East," he has not deserted you because you are living "out West." You are the deserter, and not Christ.

CHAPTER XXIX

"The water of life is free—'without money and without price,' but we must pay for pitchers to carry it in."

—Dr. Adams' "Hostess."

The Board of Church Erection has aided almost every church organization in Colorado that has a house of worship in securing the same, and, being a twin brother of the Board of Home Missions, should be liberally sustained. One of the crying needs of the Presbyterian Church to-day, that comes to us from all over our beloved land, is more money for church buildings.

Hundreds of homeless churches are struggling for life because they are homeless. A church organization without a church building is like a family without a home—no certain abiding-place. In many instances they worship God as a church when it is most convenient for the owners of the building to allow it to be used for that purpose (the use of it for other purposes paying the owners better). The consequence is, such organizations without church buildings do not become strong; rarely are they self-supporting. True, the Board supplements the minister's salary and the field is "held"; but when, with the aid of our Board of Church Erection, a comfortable house of worship is erected and the homeless organization housed, then the field is not only "held," but the work progresses; and if there be a reasonable growth in the town, the church becomes self-supporting, and not only releases the Board of Home Missions from paying part of the minister's salary, but is a source of help in assisting feeble churches by its contributions. Every dollar contributed to the Board of Church Erection brings returns such as should encourage the contributor to invest more in the same way.

There is something like speculation in nearly everything in life. Even in our giving we find objects which appear worthy; yet in giving to them we are taking chances. But there are objects to which all may give with perfect freedom as to the certainty of the results; among which are the Boards of our Church, and of the latter the Board of Church Erection has ever been doing its part of the work, economically and grandly, though quietly.

While on the frontier, building churches and preaching the Gospel, I frequently wondered whether the churches so generously helped by the Board of

Church Erection would ever forget the assistance received. I think something like forgetfulness must be the case where so many churches bid an affectionate farewell to the Board of Church Erection after the church building is paid for.

CHAPTER XXX

AMUSING

"What is meant by a 'knowledge of the world' is simply an acquaintance with the infirmities of men." —*Dickens.*

A young minister once said to a prospector, "I have a prospect." Then he told how the part on which he expected to work was covered with gold, and gave a glowing description of the Heavenly Jerusalem. When he closed his description the prospector said, rather dryly: "I, too, have such a prospect, but have not been working my assessments."

A temperance lecturer visited a frontier town and, while there, delivered a lecture that was considered severe. After he had gone some one wrote him that if he would come back and deliver that lecture again he would be hanged. He replied: "Your letter received; inducements not sufficient."

While riding through Silverton, in '77, with Rev. Sheldon Jackson, D. D., we saw a sign which read:

PIONEERING IN THE SAN JUAN

"Westminster Saloon." I asked the Doctor if he "thought that was kept by a Presbyterian?"

A friend introduced me to a gentleman who had bought an interest in a small smelter. After the purchase had been made by the company to which he belonged, the majority felt that it was not the proper thing to be engaged in a business that necessitated working on the Sabbath. The man's conscience seemed to be troubling him. He explained how they came to purchase the smelter, and then added that the members of the company had decided to devote one-seventh of the profits to charitable work. Said he: "What do you think about it, Mr. Darley?" The man, having asked a pointed question, was deserving of a pointed answer. I said: "I can tell you a story that contains the whole business." "All right," said he. "An Assyrian, after his conversion, refused to work on the Sabbath day. His employer remonstrated with him, saying that the Bible taught that if a man's ass fell into a pit on the Sabbath lay it was right to pull him out. 'Yes,' said the Assyrian, 'but if the same ass falls into the same pit every Sabbath, you had better sell the ass or fill up the pit.'" After thinking a moment, my new acquaintance said:

AMUSING

"You are right, that story puts it all into a nut-shell."

A miner died while the "Parson" was away from camp and, after a consultation held by his friends, it was decided not to bury him without appropriate remarks. An educated, though somewhat dissipated friend was chosen to "conduct services." The friend said among other things: "The departed was a noble specimen of mankind; high-minded, brave and true, a man of generous impulses; since he came among us he was never known to drink alone."

On one occasion when the "Parson" asked to hold services in a saloon, the proprietor not only consented, but generously proposed to "ring up" the loose men in the small camp. After procuring a dinner bell from the log-cabin hotel, he rang the bell vigorously while walking from cabin to cabin, at the same time crying loudly: "All you ungodly, sinning ———, come and hear the Gospel preached!"

When the service was over the "Parson" received a very gratifying contribution.

A San Juan miner sold a mine in New York and, feeling rich, went into a leading restaurant and ordered dinner. Being dressed in Western style, little attention was paid to him. As a waiter passed, the miner said: "Bring me something to eat." The waiter replied: "I am serving a fifty-dollar dinner." The miner then exclaimed: "Bring me a fifteen-hundred-dollar dinner of ham and eggs!"

CHAPTER XXXI

A FEW THOUGHTS WHILE ON THE TRAIL

"Thinking is creating with God, as thinking is writing with the ready writer; and worlds are only leaves turned over in the process of composition about His throne." —*Beecher.*

The religion of Christ, as presented to us in His life, and manifested in the lives of His faithful followers, who daily live in the Spirit and walk as the Spirit directs, is the most beautiful thing of which the human mind can conceive. For it is not only heaven-born in its teachings and tendencies, but it lifts the soul of man upward as nothing else can. It sustains in life, comforts in death, and through Jesus will usher the soul that believes into heavenly joys that will never end.

Sorrows and afflictions always carry with them a cup of ointment made up of God's mercy and love. If we ask God for his Holy Spirit, He will grant our request; and when the Comforter is come, He will apply the ointment to the bruised hearts and cause them to be healed.

PIONEERING IN THE SAN JUAN

Sometimes God in His infinite wisdom sees it is for man's best good and His own glory to pluck the bud and take it to Himself, which if left to bloom on earth would be the most beautiful of all the roses on the bush. Mourning one, comfort your troubled heart, and look up; for so sure as God plucked the rose in the bud, just so sure will He cause it to bloom in the garden of that heavenly paradise above.

Christianity can never grow and flourish under the shadow of worldliness any more than can corn under the shadow of forest trees. One needs the Sun of Righteousness, the other the sun in the firmament, that they may grow and bear fruit; one for the glory of God, the other for the benefit of man. If we conform to the world, we become shrouded with its darkness, and our light will not shine through the mist that surrounds us. Instead of our light shining that others, seeing our good works, may glorify God, we put our light under a bushel and give no light to the world.

Many who reject Christ now and try to overthrow His kingdom, like those who were determined that He should die the death of a malefactor, are as conscious of the hard task they have undertaken, and work as zealously for the accomplishment of their terrible purpose, as did the false accusers of our blessed Lord.

The windows of the soul are often clouded by tears that fall from our eyes, because many relatives and friends have crossed the dark river; and for that reason even the most precious promises and cheering truths in God's word are seen "through a glass darkly"; therefore lose much of their strength and sweetness for a while; but when God in mercy wipes clean those windows we not only see but realize the strength and comfort contained in His promises, and are cheered by the God-given truth, "Blessed are the dead that die in the Lord."

God, who sitteth in the heavens, and judgeth all mankind, is not controlled in His judgment by the impatience of His creatures regarding His time and way of rendering unto every man his just dues. "Shall not the Judge of all the earth do right?" Neither is He controlled in His judgment of what is best for His children by their anxiety and ignorance as to what is for their best good. "Your Father knoweth what things ye have need of."

PIONEERING IN THE SAN JUAN

Strong faith in God, faith that causes His children to lie calmly, contentedly and peacefully in His arms, enjoying religion as they are privileged, comes not without experience, for in religion, as in other things, experience is needed. The ripe experience that comes through trial often proves a great blessing. By experience we learn that God will not do for us what we can do for ourselves, and that He delights to be inquired of. It would be injurious to our souls for God to place His loving and protecting hand between us and some trial we are approaching, for the experience brought may be just what the soul needs. Should God always stand between us and trial we might come to believe that by our own wisdom we had avoided it. To be truly benefited by God's mercies we must learn by experience to appreciate what God in mercy sends.

Put all the love that is possible into your faith, and you will not find it difficult to serve God. Love smooths the roughest edges of obedience, and makes the hardest work for the Master a pleasure.

A log cabin with a dirt roof is the most comfortable house that can be built. It is coolest in summer and warmest in winter. Whenever we hear those who are living in elegant-looking and finely-painted houses, with shingled or slated roof, complaining of the heat in summer, or the cold in winter, we feel that it is a pleasant thing to have a log cabin, with a dirt roof, to live in. Not every one can stand all these comforts without becoming proud, but some can. While the log-cabinites have reason to feel proud, their sympathy for their suffering and unfortunate fellow citizens who are compelled to live in houses made of board or of brick, and then shingled over, keeps them from organizing what might be called the log-cabin aristocracy. And since we are not proud and do not like to be called by big-sounding names, nor cold-hearted enough to laugh at the unfortunate, we log-cabinites will just enjoy our log cabins and keep still about it.

CHAPTER XXXII

"Ye lame, fear not, you will not be cast out. Two snails entered the ark; how they got there I cannot tell. It must have taken them a long time. They must have set off rather early, unless it be that Noah took them part of the way. So some of you are snails; you are on the right road; but it will take a long while, unless some blessed Noah helps you into the ark."
                                                              —*Spurgeon.*

The trouble is not, as some have supposed, the inability of home missionaries to preach acceptably, but the live-on-father-as-long-as-we-can spirit that is in so many mission churches. When a church building is to be erected, the first question asked is, "How much can we get from the Board of Church Erection?" When the missionary's salary is mentioned, the first question asked is, "How much will the Board of Home Missions give us?" Having had some experience in home mission work, I know whereof I speak.

This live-on-father-as-long-as-we-can spirit is, to say the least, a spirit that should be despised, whether it be in a church or individual. It has often brought trial to the home of some faithful missionary. He is conscientious, knows something of the great work that is being done, and the usually low financial condition of the Board, tries his best to have the church or churches to which he preaches take care of themselves, since he is unwilling that more should be asked of the board than is necessary, and since the Board can only pay out what is paid in, he suffers to no small extent. "But," says one, "educate the members of these churches up to a higher standard of Christian duty." Correct! Those who serve these lame home mission churches are trying to do this, and therefore are on the "right road"; but it will take these churches a long time to become self-supporting "unless some blessed Noah helps them into the ark." After a man has spent years in home-mission work on the frontier, and has been taught by experience that about the time he begins to see a little fruit for his labor in that direction the members of his church and congregation (or the majority of them) depart for newer, greener and richer fields, where churches are scarcer and money reported to be more plentiful, he feels that the educating process goes very slow. Home missionaries are compelled to face another discouraging fact. Out West many sit Sabbath after Sabbath without contributing to the support of

the church, beyond a mere trifle for the defraying
of contingent expenses, while they are paying hand-
some prices for pews in self-supporting churches
"back East." They claim their letters are there,
or their families occupy the pews; therefore they are
not able to pay toward the support of missionaries
out West. And yet they do contribute toward this
cause through the collections taken in their home
churches. I have thought at times, when looking
over the "Minutes of the General Assembly," that
some of the churches back East were afflicted with
lameness toward home missions, large member-
ships and the column for "Congregational
Expenses" showing that much was annually
expended for the support of their own churches, yet
very little contributed toward home missions.
What is needed in the majority of churches all over
the land is less lameness and more of the Holy
Spirit. "As a ship in the midst of the sea goeth not
toward the haven unless it have a prosperous gale of
wind, even so the church of God goeth not to its
wished-for haven unless it be blown with the Spirit
of God, and directed and set on by the same Spirit."

CHAPTER XXXIII

"The blossom cannot tell what becomes of its odor, and no man can tell what becomes of his influence and example that roll away from him and go beyond his ken on their perilous mission."   —*Beecher*.

No matter how hard a minister of the Gospel may have labored or how many hardships he may have endured, he cannot leave a field where he has worked for years without thoughts that cause his heart to be filled with heaviness, and his eyes with tears.   Yet, if he has been faithful, and has done his utmost to advance the Master's kingdom among men, he will be remembered.   Even the "queer class" will not forget him, and when eternity dawns he will realize that "much of Christ's fruit is gathered in strange orchards."

Having completely broken down from exposure and overwork in the roughest portion of the Rocky Mountains, having been under a severe strain for nearly five years, I was compelled to give up a work that was very dear to my heart.   When my few household goods were nearly packed, I was

called upon by two of my "peculiar friends."
Without any preliminaries one of them began piling
up silver dollars and five-dollar bills on a little
table. When the money was counted, the one
who had brought it said: "Mr. Darley, there is one
hundred and thirty-seven dollars from the boys; not
one cent is from a church member. You have given
us hell for five years; but you have always given it
to us in the teeth. You have been kind to us when
we were sick, and never said one word against the
dead. We are sorry you are going away and this is
to show our appreciation."

The earnestness of the speaker, although under
the influence of liquor, and the fact that he had been
brought up in a Christian home, caused me to see
that the good seed sown in his heart long years
before still struggled to grow and bear fruit; but
years of wandering from his father's house amid the
dark mountains of sin had marred and scarred his
soul. I have often asked myself what proportions
of serpent and dove should be in a Christian's heart
while dealing with these men. A quaint old minister said: "About the right proportion is an ounce
of serpent to a pound of dove." Matthew Henry
wrote: "The serpent's head (providing it be nothing akin to the old serpent) may well become a good

OURAY, COLO, LOOKING EAST IN 1898.

Christian's body, especially if it have a dove's eye in it." Dove and serpent make a rather queer combination, yet a very strong one when the right proportion enters into it.

It is difficult at times to tell which is the most useful to a man; for while the dove is without doubt the most beautiful, too much dove and too little serpent in any one nature would cause the possessor of it to be plucked so clean that his progress would be so slow as hardly to be perceptible. Like piety and good temper; piety, beyond doubt, is preferable to good temper without piety. A very pious elder once said to his son in view of marriage: "My boy, piety is essential for the life to come, but good temper is the requisite for happiness in this world." So would I say regarding the dove and the serpent. Dove-likeness will no doubt help a soul heavenward, yet a little of the serpent is requisite to progress in this world while dealing with all classes of men. Both are good. "Be ye therefore wise as serpents and harmless as doves."

CHAPTER XXXIV

HISTORICAL

"What histories of toils could I declare!
But still long-wearied nature wants repair." —*Pope.*

"The Presbytery of Colorado" was organized by the Enabling Act of the General Assembly at Pittsburg, Pa., November 10, 1869; on February 19, 1870, with four ministers and six churches. There had existed a "Union Presbytery" prior to this time, but it had been dissolved by the removal of the few members from the field. They are supposed to have been mostly New School Presbyterians.

"The Presbytery of Colorado" was divided by act of the Assembly at Madison, Wis., May, 1880. The division into the Presbyteries of Denver and Pueblo took place October 12, 1880, in the Central Presbyterian Church, Denver, Colorado.

"The Presbytery of Pueblo" met in the infant Sunday-school room of said church on that day and elected officers (the Moderator being Lewis Hamilton), appointed committees, and adjourned for the first regular meeting at Trinidad, April 26, 1881.

HISTORICAL

At that meeting the following ministers and churches were enrolled: Willis Lord, D. D., LL. D., Lewis Hamilton, Wm. P. Teitsworth, Jas. L. Merritt, Thos. C. Kirkwood, D. D., Ruel Dodd, John W. Partridge, Alex. M. Darley, George M. Darley, Henry B. Gage, W. W. Morton, George N. Smith, Harry L. Janeway, Achilles L. Loder, and Charles M. Shepherd; with licentiates Antonio J. Rodriguez, Juan Bautista, and candidates Manzanares and Cort —nineteen in all, of whom three were Mexicans. The churches in Pueblo Presbytery in the order of their size, and, when equal, in order of their age: Colorado Springs, Pueblo, Canon City, Trinidad, Silver Cliff, Cenicero, Lake City, Del Norte, Animas City, Salida, Rosita, Poncha Springs, Alamosa, La Jara Second, Gunnison, Ouray, San Rafael, Irwin, West Las Animas, Granada, La Jara First, Le Vata, and Saguache—twenty-three in all, with 682 members, 36 elders, and 11 deacons. Three of these churches were Mexican. Two more churches were ordered to be organized. At the present time (October, 1898) the First Church of Colorado Springs has a larger membership than the twenty-three churches had at the time of the organization of "The Presbytery of Pueblo," October 12, 1880. Great difficulty was experienced in getting a quorum for a meeting of Synod, and not until October 10, 1883, did we have a meeting of Synod worthy the name. Heretofore a quorum was made by a brother joining a Presbytery merely to obtain its representation. In whatever Presbytery Synod met, that Presbytery was practically Synod. But on October 10, 1883, at Del Norte, lonely Santa Fe Presbytery had three delegates, two from Santa Fe and one from Las Vegas; Denver Presbytery came down in force, and Pueblo Presbytery was with us smiling all over. Rev. George M. Darley was stated supply of the Presbyterian Church of Del Norte at that time.

At this meeting of Synod, which was the first meeting of the present "Synod of Colorado," consisting by action of the General Assembly of the Presbyteries of Denver, Pueblo and Santa Fe, a new division was made. Instead of three Presbyteries, Santa Fe was left intact; but Denver and Pueblo were divided, Boulder and Gunnison being created. This was accomplished without trouble, as the necessity of the case was recognized. One pleasant thought was apparent in all—the desire of each Presbytery to possess actual home mission ground. None of them desired to lack that noble element of the Synod's ambition and glory, the conquest of the border land for God and Presbyterianism.

HISTORICAL

Many questions of vital importance to Presbyterianism were discussed at the meeting of Synod and in the Presbyteries as they met for a short time. But the question of most importance was the location of a Presbyterian College. After propositions from various places were considered, it was decided to accept that made by the citizens of Del Norte, and it was determined to locate "The Presbyterian College of the Southwest" at that place.

When we think of the distance from any other institution of higher education, the delightful and healthful climate of the San Luis Valley, its great productiveness, untold agricultural and mineral resources, the rapidity with which the Southwest is growing, the intelligence of the settlers, their desire to educate their children, the benefit of the College to both English and Spanish-speaking people, there is no room for doubt regarding the wisdom of Synod in placing the College at Del Norte.

Josiah Copley, Esq., in an article published in the "Presbyterian Banner," has this to say for Del Norte and the Presbyterian College of the Southwest: "All seemed gratified that Del Norte was successful, for a locality more beautiful, one combining the mingled features of beauty and grandeur, or one in the midst of so large a body of soil of extraordinary productiveness, could not be found in all the Rocky Mountain region.''

A MEETING OF PUEBLO PRESBYTERY.

The Presbytery of Pueblo met in the First Presbyterian Church of Colorado Springs, Friday, April 11, 1884, at 7: 30 p. m., and was opened with a sermon by the retiring Moderator, Rev. H. B. Gage, from II. Tim., 4:1-5. There were present fifteen ministers and seven elders. Rev. Ruel Dodd was chosen Moderator, and Rev. H. Reynard temporary clerk.

The following being present, were invited to sit as corresponding members: Revs. Geo. P. Hays, D. D., Presbytery of Denver; R. C. Bristol, of the Arkansas Valley Congregational Association; A. P. Tinker, of the Presbytery of Detroit; S. H. Murphy, who has recently taken charge of the Presbyterian Church of Trinidad, from the Presbytery of Mankato; S. A. Stoddard, of the Presbytery of Neosho; J. W. Moore, of the Presbytery of Ozark, Cumberland Presbyterian Church; A. W. Arundel, of the Colorado Conference of the M. E. Church; and Elder George W. De La Verne.

From the many items of general interest the following have been selected. A call from the Del Norte church for the pastoral services of Rev. George M. Darley, promising a salary of $1,500, payable quarterly and parsonage, was presented and accepted, and the following arrangements made for the installation of the pastor-elect: Rev. Willis Lord, D. D., to preside and preach the sermon; Rev. E. McLane to charge the congregation, and Rev. J. W. Partridge to charge the pastor; the time to be arranged by correspondence with the church session and pastor-elect.

Rev. J. J. Gilchrist was given power as evangelist to receive and dismiss members in the churches of Alamosa and La Jara until such time as these churches have a session. The same power was also given to Rev. E. McLane in the churches of his field where there is no session or where it is impossible to get the session together. Elder Jas. Fullerton reported as to his work in the San Luis Valley, and his fidelity was very much commended by the brethren who were acquainted with his work.

Manuel Sanchez was continued as a teacher among the Mexicans for four months. It was also resolved to ask the Board of Home Missions to commission another lady teacher to labor in Plaza Media adjoining Miss Ross' school; also to ask $500 from the Board of Church Erection for the building of a school house at Guadalupe.

Rev. George P. Hays, D. D., informed Presbytery of the action of the Synodical Committee on Home Missions in choosing Rev. T. C. Kirkwood, D. D., as Synodical Missionary, and the Presbytery heartily voted its appreciation for the appointment of this brother to the position, though very reluctant to give up his presence and counsels in the important places which he occupies in the Presbytery.

Dr. George P. Hays also stated that the printing press of Rev. A. M. Darley had been purchased, and that a Spanish paper would soon be published at Del Norte under the editorship of Rev. E. McLane. Rev. George M. Darley and Elder George M. Stewart were elected principal delegates to the General Assembly, and Rev. T. C. Kirkwood, D. D., and Elder J. C. McLung as alternates.

The committee on publication reported that the Board was in correspondence with Rev. A. C. Gilchrist, of Vineland, Ind., with reference to taking the work of a colporteur for the Board within the bounds of the Presbytery.

On Saturday evening an important meeting was held in the interests of Home Missions, and addresses were delivered by Rev. H. B. Gage and G. M. Darley. On Sabbath evening was held a popular meeting in the interests of Foreign Missions, addressed by Rev. J. W. Partridge, of Canon City; Rev. S. H. Murphy, formerly of the Gaboon and Corisca Mission, West Africa; and Rev. E. McLane, formerly Missionary to Chile, South America. These addresses were full of interesting information, and were listened to with pleasure by a large congregation.

About noon on Monday, Presbytery adjourned, to meet in Pueblo on the Tuesday evening preceding the next regular meeting of the Synod of Colorado, which also meets in Pueblo sometime in October, the date being not yet fixed.

After a pleasant and harmonious meeting, the brethren separated to return to their various fields of labor, but not without expressing their hearty thanks to the good people of Colorado Springs for their royal entertainment of the Presbytery.

CHAPTER XXXV

A QUEER WAY OF LOOKING AT DEATH

"There is generally something that requires hiding at the bottom of a mystery." —*Hawthorne.*

Man is a queer animal—when left to grow up without care, uneducated, and trod upon in his youth and early manhood. A specimen of this kind called at my home in company with a girl that had worked for us. The poor girl was in great sorrow, and had been for several months. Her mother had been an invalid; her step-father was animal in large degree. One night the mother disappeared very mysteriously. The husband was arrested amid considerable feeling that was unpleasant for him. Three months after the disappearance of the mother, her bones were found in "The Great River of the North."

The coroner's jury held an inquest over the remains, after which the daughter desired the funeral services to be held at the undertaker's. She came to see about the funeral with a friend of the family who was the worse for liquor. Being a queer animal, he put things in rather a queer way.

QUEER WAY OF LOOKING AT DEATH

He was indignant that any "fuss" had been made over the matter in the first place. He said: "I yest tell you vat it tise, Mr. Darley, I believe dot ven any one vants to die like dot vomans did, it makes not difrence vich road dey go; by the river" (it was claimed she had drowned herself) "or by some other road. It vas yest so goot to go dot vay as any other vay; but before she go, vy don't she yest write somedings on a piece of paper, and say she vas going dot vay, and save all dis hell of a fuss?" The poor girl sat still, but looked as though the explanation was not just as she would have liked; yet the funeral services were held, and she seemed satisfied. The husband did not attend the funeral, but sent word that "some one had to stay on the ranch to keep the cattle from eating up the crop."

CHAPTER XXXVI

"Extremes meet when expediency renders it desirable."
—*Round Table.*

At Del Norte, years ago, we had some men who were not considered good citizens, and the county contained a few more of like character. One in particular was not loved by the ranchmen, because he was accused of counting more cattle for his own than belonged to him.

After repeated attempts to make him feel the force of law, and having failed every time, they decided to try lynch-law. The man was no fool and always appeared to me to be a perfect gentleman. I do not think that his worst enemy would say he was not gentlemanly in his bearing. A stranger standing by while he talked to the minister would have taken him for one of the "pillars of the church," from the frequency of the words, "Brother Darley."

He and a man who worked for him were arrested and placed in the lower story of the little old court house, which was also used as a jail. The upper part was taken for court, town meetings, church services and other things.

On Saturday this strange character decided that he would be lynched and made all preparations for it; that is, such as he considered necessary, even to the placing of his watch in charge of someone. Then he and his hired man waited for the coming of the mob. A strong guard had been placed around the building. Saturday night wore away, but no mob came. While services were being held Sabbath evening, guards were about armed with rifles. The audience seemed a trifle nervous; but the hall was well filled and the services closed on time. All knew that the mob would not fire into the building while church was in session. Monday night I heard the mob passing my house and listened to the first blow that was struck against the great clasp that held the jail door. Almost immediately the firing began and it was claimed that over one hundred shots were discharged. It was not the intention of the mob to do any shooting; they intended to take both men out quietly, as had been the "Lee Roy Brothers" in previous years, and hang them, possibly to the same tree.

The notorious one afterwards told me that it was

like this: "When my partner and I heard the mob coming I said to him: 'Let us get right up close to the door, and the moment the lock is broke, let us throw the door open and run for our lives; put your head down and jump right into the crowd. You run to the left and I will run to the right.'" This they did, and it was not what the mob expected. The hired man was killed, but the other made his escape. It was a moonlight night, and he told me: "I could see where the balls struck my shadow."

He was afterwards shot in the leg, brought back, tried and acquitted. Then, in a few years, he was shot in the neck and chest. The sheriff used a shotgun at short range. This happened in the night, near where my boys were camping. But after he was shot the sheriff and his men did not dare go along the road, knowing the desperate character of the man, and they were wise in their action. He waited to kill them, and finally took the saddle from the animal he was riding, saddled his own mule and rode some distance to a ranch, where he went to bed, and was found the next morning weak from the loss of blood.

The next night after the mob attempted to lynch both men and only succeeded in killing one, I picked up two bullets from my pulpit; they had gone through the siding and the plastering. Then they struck the ceiling and dropped upon the pulpit. I have them now.

CHAPTER XXXVII

A BURRO TAKES PART IN CHURCH SERVICE

"The devil cannot stand music." *—Luther.*

It is often said that ministers' children are mischievous. I do not see why they should differ from those of other men, unless they be more patient because frequently compelled to wait a long while for what they need by reason of the fact that the salary of the minister is slow in coming into his possession.

I confess, however, to having one son who enjoys the ludicrous as well as most boys, and said boy at one time owned one of the most knowing and musical "Rocky Mountain canaries" that it has been my privilege to see or hear. If it could get loose from its lariat when the boys were out camping, it would eat up their dinner and then remain near the cart until they came for their meal; then look abused when punished for eating the "grub."

One Sabbath evening I noticed that the burro was hitched to a post near the back window of the church. I said to Ward: "Take that burro and tie it farther away from the church, for if you don't, just as soon as I commence preaching it will begin braying.'' Ward replied, "Maud" (that was the burro's name) "has been better trained than that." Believing in good training, I said no more.

Maud gave me a decidedly friendly look as I passed her on my way to the church, as if to say: "Parson, I'll do what I can to help you out to-night." Sure enough, when I was well into my sermon, "Maud" began. First a solo—low, clear, penetrating, not altogether unmusical; then a kind of duet, the outgoing breath making one sort of noise, the incoming another. This was followed by a quartet, composed of the most hideous noises that it was possible for one of her species to make. By that time I had stopped; but "Maud," true to her nature, continued. The congregation could not contain themselves; for the burros of the neighborhood began answering, and I really think from the way that "Maud" then let out her voice that she thought it was an encore. The boy was in the congregation, and looked as though he wished that burro out of the country; for no minister's son would intentionally have his father interrupted while preaching.

At times the burro does as the owner wishes,

again otherwise. "Maud" once took it into her head to cross the D. & R. G. Railroad track as the train was coming; and having determined to do so, her owners saved her life and theirs by jumping on the shafts of the cart and, by the use of one line and the long ears of the burro, guided her into a fence as the train rushed by within a few feet.

Burros are not noted for either brains or fear, unless it be fear of wild animals. One night during the early days of the San Juan excitement a mountain lion was prowling around my camp. The burro I then had was a big "jack," but he was so frightened that he would stand with his head over my body. By the light of the campfire I could see that he was trembling like a "leaf of a tree."

CHAPTER XXXVIII

TWO MEN LYNCHED

"Death tarries not in its approach to the unfortunate and the abandoned." —*Miss Annie E. Dickenson.*

On general principles we condemn lynch-law; first, as being in itself a breaking of the law and a crime against good government; second, as setting a bad example to the rising generation; and third, as giving an excuse to bad men to take the law into their own hands that they may wreak their vengeance upon men who do not deserve hanging.

Yet every man who has seen much of frontier life will, I think, agree with me when I say that hanging is the only thing that will make some men quit their cussedness.

Hinsdale County, of which Lake City is the county seat, had one of the best sheriffs that ever held that office in Colorado. A man as kindly in his disposition as he was brave, as ready to assist the needy as he was to assist his own family—the one man who had helped me do a large part of the rough carpenter work on our first church over the range, free of charge. Mr. Campbell was a credit to our camp.

One night he was murdered, while doing his duty as an officer of the law, by about as vile a specimen of humanity as could be found. This murderer, together with a pal named "Shortie," was captured, tried in the minds of the people, found worthy of death, and hanged. So far as I know, everyone lynched in southwestern Colorado, during my residence in that part of the state for nearly thirteen years, deserved all they received. True, many were killed in a way that looked as though the law was taken out of the hands of the officers and put into the hands of those who went for the law-breakers.

This same sheriff once invited me to capture an escaped criminal. He asked if I was going over into the Animas country, a distance of one hundred miles, over as rough a trail as could be found in the Rocky Mountains. I replied that was my intention. Said he: "It is a long, hard trip, and I don't care to go on uncertainties. I have information that a hard character" (who had escaped, giving his name) "is in that country. If you will bring him back with you I will see that you are well paid for your trouble; I know you can do it if you will." Ministers who are going through a country looking after the organization of churches in new settlements are not liable to spend their time looking for escaped law-breakers. I always went well armed, but not for that purpose. There was something that occurred during the height of the excitement of the first great rush that seemed absolutely necessary for the success of church work and good order; this caused the sheriff to make the proposition; but a work of necessity for a minister or a sheriff is quite different.

CHAPTER XXXIX

A WISE WALK.

"The introduction of a discourse should be a rifle-shot at the theme." *—Rev. W. M. Paxton, D.D.*

The following sermon was preached by the Author in the Central Presbyterian Church of Denver, Colorado, April 11, 1893, as retiring Moderator of Denver Presbytery:

TEXT (COLOSSIANS 4: 5.):

"Walk in wisdom toward them that are without."

Because a command is difficult to obey it does not lessen its force or release us from our duty, providing the command be given by one who has the right to give it. We consider it right to obey the commands of earthly rulers, when they are given for the good of the nation to which we belong. This is right, for it has the word of God for its foundation. "The powers that be are ordained of God," and should be obeyed.

In our text we have a command given by one who has the right to command, and because we have found from past experience that there is difficulty in obeying, that does not lessen the force of the command nor our obligation to try, by God's help, to obey.

"Walk in wisdom toward them that are without."

Like the church at Colosse, to whom these words were written, we are surrounded by many who do not believe as we do, who have not accepted the Lord Jesus Christ as their ruler; but who say, "This man shall not rule over us." We come in contact with them daily; they are in our homes, among our associates; sometimes they are intimate friends, beloved because of their nobleness and generosity; often they are partners in life with those who are followers of Christ; thousands of them are the children of pious parents, while many are the baptized children of the church.

True, all is not darkness around us, nor are we surrounded with just the same class of people that the Colossians were; yet we find much that ought not to be passed by unnoticed. Occasionally we find dwelling under the same roof persons of such opposite tastes, views, and education, that to hear them talk you would suppose there were gods many and saviors not a few; and you are soon convinced that one follows the true God, while of the other you can truthfully say, he is a follower of strange gods.

We may say, this is not as it should be; this is not as we would like to see it; this shows that all are not walking in that straight and narrow path which leads heavenward; but on the contrary many are walking in the broad way which leadeth to destruction. We should bear in mind that a dislike of what we see and what we know to be wrong in others will not convince them of their error. Our words and actions when coming from the heart and blessed of God, and not our dislikes, will lead those who are in the wrong to see their error and forsake their evil ways.

Of the many stubborn facts that we have to face in this world I have mentioned but a few. What are we going to do about all this? How are we going to help society? How are we going to elevate those who need it? We are told in our text to walk "wisely toward them"; not to shun them; not to treat those who are "without" as though we were better than they by nature; but show that we are better by grace, by what our acceptance, faith in, and association with Christ, love for, and communion with God, and the proper treatment of the heavenly guest, who dwells in our hearts, has made us. Paul acted wisely in his day toward those who were without. "And unto the Jews I became as a Jew, that I might gain the Jews; to them that are under the law, as under the law, that I might gain them that are under the law; to them that are without law, as without law, (being not without law to God, but under the law to Christ), that I might gain them that are without law. To the weak became I as weak, that I might gain the weak; I am made all things to all men, that I might by all means save some."

"And this I do for the Gospel's sake." We see by this that Paul was willing, in all reasonable and right matters, to conform to the wishes of the people. It was not from fear, for Paul was a brave man; but for the "Gospel's sake," that he might lawfully benefit those with whom he associated, whether they were within or "without." Verily, he walked wisely.

By an examination of our hearts we discover that we are not perfect; and should this examination be with a view to bringing ourselves to see our duty toward those around us, we will see that it is wrong to allow dislikes to hinder us in our walk "toward them that are without." "Walking wisely" does not mean pharisaically, ostentatiously, or unkindly; neither are we to conclude that it means to pass by on the other side, as did the Levite, look at them, and then pass them by; but to walk "in newness of life," "worthy of the vocation wherewith ye are called"; walk circumspectly, with one object in view—the glory of God and the good of our fellow men.

If we would "walk wisely" toward "them that are without," we must walk charitably toward one another; with brotherly love; in honor preferring one another. "Not minding high things, but condescending to men of low estate;" neither will we "be wise in our own conceit." But someone may say it is easier to preach than to practice; how am I to get the wisdom that will enable me to "walk wisely toward them that are without"? The true and only way is recorded in God's word: "If any of you lack wisdom, let him ask of God, that giveth to all men liberally and upbraideth not, and it shall be given him."

It is extremely difficult to tell just where we should draw the line that will remind us that we are to walk kindly, courteously, unselfishly and hospitably "toward them that are without," and at the same time carefully—yea, even cautiously—lest we be led to walk with them instead of walking wisely toward them. We, of ourselves, are not able to lay down rules by which to go, but God has done so in His word. Be careful and guarded in all your conversation with the world, neither adopt questionable customs. For "evil communications corrupt good manners." Sit not in "the seat of the scornful," go not with the multitude to do evil. Be careful not to hurt the feelings of anyone, nor increase their prejudice against religion; neither give anyone an occasion of dislike. Our object should ever be the same—to do them all the good we can. May our speech be seasoned with salt and our discourse be such as becometh Christians; not making ourselves and our religion displeasing to them; not forcing our religion upon them. Yet, "be ye always ready to give an answer to every man who asketh you a reason for the hope that is in you with meekness and fear."

By examining our text we see that "walking wisely toward them that are without" includes walking wisely toward them that are within. For, if we walk unwisely toward them that are within, how, let me ask, are we to walk wisely toward them that are "without"? The root of wise action must be well watered by the graces that make our lives beautiful to them that are within ere the fruit of wise action will appear to them that are "without."

PIONEERING IN THE SAN JUAN

Probably we would see more fruit for our labor
should we bear in mind continually that our every
act, whether it be wise or unwise, is noticed by our
heavenly Father; and that most of our acts, wise or
unwise, are noticed by our fellow men; for, as the
apostle tells us, "we are made a spectacle to the
world, and to angels, and to men." This being
true, should we not give heed to the words of our
text? "The church of God is like a city of which all
believers are the inhabitants, connected with each
other by mutual relationship." Our walls are seen
by the inhabitants of this world, and our confession
causes us to be marked by them; we, by our profession, claim to be "children of light." We who
are within know this, and so do those who are
"without" Should we be ashamed of this? Should
we try to walk among God's people in such a way
that those who are in the church of Christ cannot
distinguish us from the worldling? In a word, shall
we "let our light shine," or shall we "hide it under
a bushel"? If we are letting our light shine we are
acting wisely and justly toward them that are without; for they have great need of our assistance;
they need to be made willing to be led, and then
led in such a way as not to become disgusted with
their leader. I know nothing that requires more

wisdom than is needed in our walk toward those who make no profession of religion. If we fall in the presence of those who are Christ's, we wound them and cause their hearts to be grieved; but we are inside the city walls, where Christ reigns, and where charity and forbearance sit beside the judge; and where jurors are supposed, at least, to delight in mercy rather than sacrifice. But when we fall in the presence of those who make no profession of religion we not only grieve the hearts of God's children, but bring reproach upon the cause of Him we love. And while charity is often found where we least expect it, and least profession is made, yet the evil resulting from our fall may be such that a great many wise actions on the part of the prudent cannot rectify our mistake. I have often thought that the most severe test to which we are subjected in life's school of trial is that of "walking wisely toward them that are without." They try us in so many different ways and get the advantage of us so frequently, because every time we are provoked to do or say an unwise thing they have it. Those who are without judge of religion, not from the profession we make, but from the life we lead; not from what they hear preached on the Sabbath day, or from the books we place in their hands; neither do they judge of religion from what they hear of its founders, but from what they see in our lives; they judge our religion by our daily walk and conversation; they know whether or not a man's religion is swallowed up in his profession. The world's people draw the line of demarkation very plainly between what they call a wise or an unwise walk in a Christian. It often happens that they are very exacting; having made no profession they claim great latitude—but expect the followers of Christ to be almost perfect. This, at times, is rather annoying, and we think unjust; yet we must admit that we, by our profession, have said to the world, We walk on a higher plane than you do, we have been "born again," "old things are passed away; behold, all things are become new." Does not such a profession call for a wise walk toward them that are without? Walking wisely is something that we owe to God, to the Church, the world, and to our own soul. By a careful study of God's word we will be convinced that great good will result to our own souls and to the souls of those with whom we come in contact by a cheerful and ready obedience to this command.

David, in his vow of godliness, said: "I will behave myself wisely in a perfect way." David was

A WISE WALK

determined to walk wisely in everything, at home
and abroad. Have a good rule and walk by it.
Remember that the steps of a good man are
"ordered by the Lord." When David was a young
man he behaved himself wisely in all his ways, and
the Lord was with him. "Wherefore, when Saul
saw that he behaved himself very wisely, he was
afraid of him." "But all Israel and Judah loved
David, because he went out and came in before
them."

It is not enough that we walk wisely one day, or
six days in the week; but we must walk wisely
every day. Neither will any excuse that we offer
for an unwise walk be accepted by God. Our only
way is to ask pardon for the past, if our walk has
been an unwise one, and seek to walk in wisdom's
ways in the future. If it is a fact, and not a mere
profession, that the word of God is our rule, we will
be ruled by it; and if God's glory be our aim in it
all, we will find to our joy that that unseen hand is
leading us day by day, and our lives will be "hid
with Christ in God."

Walking wisely, like almost everything else, is
made easier by practice. This truth we gather
from the experience of God's children in all ages.
At first, the old man within, and temptation with-

out, caused them to take many unwise steps; but by a careful and prayerful study of God's word they saw where they failed. They saw that they had trusted to their own wisdom instead of trusting to the guidance of God's Holy Spirit; this discovery led them to seek Divine aid in their walk; and by the aid given they were enabled to walk wisely. Not only toward those who were within, but also toward those who were "without." I know that it is human to become tired of trying at times; we make good resolves, we think we are as careful as it is possible for a human being to be; we conclude that our walk is just about right, everything seems to be going straight, when all at once we make a false step. Oh! how our hearts fail us in such an hour, and how apt we are to drop our heads and take several unwise steps before we stop and raise our eyes heavenward and ask the assistance we so much need! This should not discourage, but cause us to see our continual need of Divine aid. We are in an enemy's country, and as long as life lasts we will be tried daily; our walk will be noticed and every misstep seen; and every step will influence those with whom we associate, either for good or evil. If we walk wisely "toward them that are without," we have good hope of winning them to

A WISE WALK

Christ. Our every act will be a step on which they can rise heavenward. We may think that our influence is not felt in this world, but it is; we may not be conscious of it; we may not see any good resulting from our wise walk; it may be God's will to gather in the rich, ripe, golden sheaves without our knowledge. God may see that an immediate return of what we have hoped, and for which we have prayed, would only lead us to take an unwise step. Therefore, he hides, as it were, the golden sheaves that have ripened under the good influence of our wise walk. We think at times if we could only see just what effect our walk was having upon those around us that it would be of great assistance to us. Let us stop and reverse this for one moment by asking ourselves, what effect does the walk of others have on us? What will apply to ourselves will apply to others; the same rule works both ways. If the wise walk of a neighbor or a friend is a benefit to us, let us bear in mind that a wise walk on our part will be of equal benefit to them.

We find every word in the Book of Life of great benefit in the battle of life; nothing has been placed there in vain. True, there are some passages of Scripture like great lighthouses on the shores of time, warning men, throwing light before them, and showing to the world the channel through which we must sail if we would reach that safe and quiet haven of eternal rest; but lesser lights are needed and are of greater importance than we are aware; for while they do not give as much light as some others, they guide man with equal sureness through the darkness that is around lesser temptations.

We may consider that the words of our text are like a very small light, not of much use to guide man to glory and to God; I admit that it is not as great as some others, yet if we walk in the light which a careful study of our text will give, we will find that its apparent dimness is caused by lack of appreciation on our part; the light is there, the truth is there, words of wisdom compose it. God inspired the true and faithful apostle to the Gentiles to write it, and instruction such as is needed can be found therein if we search for it. Then why not treasure it up in good and honest hearts, seeking God's help that we may obey the command given?

"Walking in wisdom toward them that are without." Life, you know, is made up of seconds, minutes, hours and days, as well as years; so our walk is made up of steps, or actions; some taken hastily, some after due consideration, yet all go toward making up our walk. This being true, how careful should we be that we are making a right use of every minute and taking a right step every time!

In conclusion, I desire to say: I hope that what has been said on the subject of walking wisely will be remembered by all who read this sermon. Every professing Christian should walk wisely, circumspectly and carefully "toward them that are without," and cordially, hospitably and peaceably toward them that are within; that we may walk with Christ while on earth, and after death dwell with him on high.

CHAPTER XL

"If I can by a lucky chance, in these days of evil, rub out one wrinkle from the brow of care, or beguile the heavy heart of one moment of sadness; if I can, now and then, penetrate the gathering film of misanthropy, prompt a benevolent view of human nature, and make my reader more in a good humor with his fellow beings and himself, surely, surely, I shall not then have written entirely in vain." — *Washington Irving*.

The following sermon was preached by the Author in the First Presbyterian Church of Colorado Springs, October 18, 1898, as retiring Moderator of the Synod of Colorado:

Subject—"No Waste in the Ministry of Love."

TEXT (St. John 12: 7.):

"Then said Jesus, Let her alone; against the day of my burying hath she done this."

It must have touched the heart of the Lord Jesus when Mary anointed his feet, and then wiped them with her hair. And while Judas tried to make out that there had been a waste, Jesus let his disciples know that "against the day of his burying she kept this," and has taught his followers that there is no waste in the ministry of love. I believe there may be mistakes, yet in this blessed ministry there can be no waste; and undoubtedly there are fewer mistakes in love's ministry than in any other. I do not believe that "love is blind," although many things are credited to love that are devoid of soundness, but when traced to the proper source prove to be the acts of an almost insane jealousy. Ignorance often ignores the ministry of love and claims that some of the noblest sacrifices made by men and women are a waste of time, talents and means; but the fault lies with those who make the criticism, and not with those who do the work, make the sacrifices, and love the Master.

Among all the kindnesses shown our Lord by those who dwelt in that hospitable home in Bethany, by Martha, Mary and Lazarus, I believe that this kindness done by Mary was the greatest and appreciated the most by him. The preciousness of the ointment surely had its value in the eyes of our Savior, yet the love that crowned the gift was valued a thousand-fold more. Water and a coarse towel would have answered the purpose for bathing and wiping the feet of Jesus on ordinary occasions; but now that the time was approaching when the feet of our Lord would be nailed to the cross, there was nothing too precious with which to bathe them, and a woman's hair, which is her glory, was not too sacred to be used in the place of a towel. There are times when there should be an outlay of that which is precious, yea, times when we should show our love for the Savior by giving to him that which is of the greatest value; even life, if that becomes necessary. There are times when we should give that which is precious to those on earth.

We are not told how wide was the circle of Mary's acquaintances, nor how influential she was in society. But we are told how she loved Jesus, and so long as the world stands, her great act of love will remain as evidence that there is no waste in the ministry of love. Had Mary been the wife or the daughter of an earthly king, her influence in her day might have been far wider for good or evil; but how soon would she have been forgotten! and now instead of her name being mentioned in loving remembrance wherever the Gospel of Christ is preached, it would have been locked fast in the past. A narrow wall, so far as earthly fame in Palestine went, had been built around Mary. Yet by the ministry of love that wall has been extended, until to-day it encircles the world. Love built that wall, and the strength of Jehovah defends it; therefore the gates of hell shall not prevail against it. "Verily I say unto you, wheresoever this Gospel shall be preached in the whole world, there shall this also, that this woman hath done, be told for a memorial of her."

Evidently the ointment Mary used on this occasion was rare and difficult to obtain, "of great value"; but in her eyes nothing was too valuable to be used for the comfort, or the glory of her Lord.

Since the day that the words of the text were spoken, great changes have come over the face of the earth; barren wastes have been made to blossom like the rose; while part of the earth that was highly cultivated then is almost a desert now. The channels of rivers have changed. Nations that were not in existence then have become the leading nations of the world. Change is written everywhere. Yet with all the changes written across earth's face, no change has come to the hearts of men; they are still deceitful above all things and desperately wicked; with here and there an oasis of love for some human being, if not for God, in every heart; with some here and others in different places who do have a high appreciation of all that is true, pure and soul-ennobling, firmly believing and acting on their belief in the blessed truth that there is no waste in the ministry of love.

How often do we hear men, to whom we had given credit of knowing better, speak of the waste there is both in money and men in the great work of foreign missions, and in the equally great work of home missions! Those of intelligence speak of the waste of life and property that has been cheerfully laid upon our country's altar. But believe it, no matter how much of that which is dear to the hearts of true men and women may be laid upon God's altar, or our country's altar, there is no waste when it helps to fill out the ministry of love.

Speaking of the "alabaster box of very precious ointment" which Mary broke, and of her knowledge of that "decease" of which Christ spoke so frequently, as well as her love for Jesus, one has said: "It is not unreasonable to suppose, remembering the fondness of Jewish women for such perfumes, that Mary may have had that alabaster box of very costly ointment from olden days, before she had learned to serve Christ; then, when she came to know him, and must have learned how constantly that decease, of which he ever spoke, was before his mind, she may have put it aside, 'kept it against the day of his burying.'" To me this would be just like a woman; to keep a thing until love suggested it was time to use it. How often our mothers did that! How often do those who are dearer than life to our hearts do the same thing now—keep something for us, precious because it has been kept till the right time, as well as precious in itself, and then lovingly bestow it upon us!

Probably Mary knew better than any other follower of Jesus that his earthly ministry would soon cease. She may have been aware that this anointing was "against the day of his burying," before Jesus told his disciples in her presence that it was. If so, then beyond doubt her faith made it a twofold anointing—that of the best guest of the feast and that of preparation for that burial which of all others she apprehended was so terribly near. And deep humility now offered what earnest love had provided, and intense faith, in view of what was coming, applied. And so she poured ointment over his head, over his feet; then, stooping down, wiped them with her hair, as if not only in evidence of service and love, but in fellowship of his death. "And the house was filled"—and to all time his house, the church, is filled "with the odor of the ointment."

Waste this was in the eyes of the disciples, but not waste in the eyes of Mary's Lord, and of our Lord, because it was a service of love, and great was Mary's reward. And believe it, dear hearers, great will be our reward, if we render unto Jesus the service of love. For the harder we work in the Master's vineyard now, the sweeter will be the rest in the house of the Master by and by, when earthly labors cease and heavenly joys begin.

Jesus said: "Let her alone," and to-day he says to every opposer of his cause, and to every one in his church who is disposed to criticise acts of love for the Master, just because they do not coincide with their view: "Let my workers alone." "Hinder me not," said the faithful servant when he had been convinced that Rebekah was the proper person to become his master's wife, and "Hinder me not," has been the cry of many a faithful servant of the great Master, in all ages; while those who have no particular interest in the upbuilding of his kingdom hinder them in their work in so many ways. One way is by constantly crying: "To what purpose is this waste?" Oh, why do you do as you do? Why don't you do as we wish you to do? Yes, regarding all who are breaking their precious box of ointment at the Master's feet, Jesus says to every fault-finder: "Let them alone—they have a good purpose in doing as they do, and the smell of the ointment is very sweet to me. You may not appreciate the efforts they are making to honor me, but I do. Let them alone; for against the day of my coming again, when 'all the tribes of the earth shall mourn, and they shall see the Son of Man coming in the clouds of heaven with power and great glory,' they are doing this."

Love's ministry was appreciated by our Savior before his crucifixion and burial, and it was appreciated by him after his resurrection, when those faithful women went early unto the tomb where their Lord had been laid. When he comes again he will abundantly reward every one who has shown love for him in any way.

When we first read of Christ's approval of Mary's loving act, we are liable to think that the Savior approves of outward display when his children seek to honor him; but, when we consider the matter carefully, we are convinced that this was no ordinary occasion; no ordinary service; one which ought to be commonly used in the church. This act of Mary, we are plainly told, was in connection with his burial.

The Savior frequently enjoins us to be sober and moderate in the use of everything that leads toward that which is carnal, or only an outward observance of the worship of God. "God is a spirit, and they that worship Him must worship Him in spirit and in truth." I am aware of the fact that many would have us believe that in the breaking of the alabaster box and in the anointing of Jesus with the precious ointment it contained, we find a lesson taught; that costly and magnificent worship is pleasing to God. But men everywhere are ready to grasp and hold that which pleases the senses rather than that which is spiritual and benefits the soul. This accounts in part for the crowds that gather (upon the Lord's day) in places of amusement, or in places where their tastes are pleased, and for the few (comparatively speaking) who prefer going where they will hear the plain, unvarnished Gospel preached. "Wasting your time!" is their cry, when told we prefer the simple Gospel truths before that which suits the fancy and pleases the senses, but starves the soul. No one who loves the Lord Jesus, and desires to take part in the ministry of love, will say that the anointing of Jesus by Mary, and the wiping of his feet with her hair, were superfluous; for he was soon to be buried; and this, I believe, was done under the direction of God's Spirit, for He has influenced His children in many ways and on many occasions ever since the beginning of time, and will continue to do so until time shall end.

What was proper for Mary to do to her Lord,

THE MINISTRY OF LOVE

"against the day of his burying," would not be the proper thing for his followers to do now to one another; and while all tenderness and love should be shown toward the living and the dead, let us keep in mind, as we think of all that Jesus accomplished by his death, resurrection and ascension, the great blessing brought to our souls by believing in Him; that "the odors of his resurrection have now sufficient efficacy, without spikenard and costly ointment, to quicken the whole world." Also keep in mind that everything that we have belongs to the One who died for our sins and rose for our justification, and who now maketh intercession for us before His Father and our Father in heaven.

Let us emphasize what I have already said: There may be mistakes in the ministry of love, yet no waste, that our charity may become very broad toward all who desire to honor the Lord Jesus Christ. We are not all constituted alike, nor have all been educated in just the same way; consequently, what one may consider the best thing to do that Christ's name may be honored, others equally sincere and equally anxious to honor the Savior may not think best. Therefore, let us be careful lest we fall into error in our judgment regarding one another. We are not expected to give up our Christian liberty, nor should we ask that others give up theirs; and while retaining our own and permitting others to keep theirs, let us not be saying we are right and careful not to waste what belongs to our Lord, implying that those who differ from us are wasting that which should be used for the honor of God's name and the upbuilding of his kingdom. If any one, while trying to serve God honestly, makes mistakes (and who does not make mistakes?), let us not censure nor discourage him; but the rather help him—or at least let him alone.

The disciples put an unfavorable construction upon Mary's act, that was so filled with love, while Jesus approved it. And I believe that at the present day many acts of love, approved by the Savior, are disapproved by men who, like His disciples of old, really love Him. We pride ourselves on being good judges of human nature, yet we know that we cannot read what is in a man's heart (God alone can do that); and while we may read faces, we cannot interpret acts of love as they should be interpreted. Therefore, men will continue to misunderstand one another and misjudge one another and consider very much wasted what in reality is a sweet-smelling savor to God, and will, in that last great day, stand forth as something none will then be ashamed to acknowledge as a part of the good work of the true ministry of love.

In the battle of life we find very much to try our faith, our patience and our love; and some of us may have natures that are hard to control. We find that the old man will persist in asserting himself, even while we are engaged in the Master's service, trying to honor Him. Many have been wounded in days that have long since passed away, and those wounds, while healed, have left deep scars. Therefore, as we journey heavenward, let us be kindly and affectionate toward one another, remembering that, "when a scar cannot be taken away, the next kind office is to hide it." "Then said Jesus, Let her alone: against the day of my burying hath she kept this." She meant well; and in Christ's sight, and in reality, there was no waste, because in the ministry of love there can be none.

At times I have wondered whether this Mary was naturally diffident or whether she was inclined to let her affections be known (most likely the former), for I believe, with Ruskin, that "the best women are indeed necessarily the most difficult to know; they are recognized chiefly in the happiness of their husbands and the nobleness of their children. They are only to be divined, not discerned, by the stranger and sometimes seem almost helpless except in their homes." But let this be as it may, we know that Jesus appreciated what Mary did. And to-day He appreciates the ministry of love in which so many faithful women are engaged, as well as the work performed by His embassadors. Were it not true that we have the immutable word of God for it, that "the work of a man shall He render unto him, and cause every man to find according to his ways," the large majority of His laborers would find but little to encourage them to continue in the work.

"The best things in this world are not the best things God provides for his children." Humanly speaking, the opposite is generally true. And occasionally his embassadors see the same spirit which was manifested toward Christ while he was in the flesh. One day they cried, "Hosanna!" and another day they cried, "Crucify him!" Yet, after all, we recognize the points in Whitcomb Riley's "Philosophy":

"The signs is bad when folks commence
A findin' fault with Providence,
And balkin' 'cause the earth don't shake
At ev'ry prancing step they take.

THE MINISTRY OF LOVE

No man is great till he can see
How less than little he would be
Ef stripped to self, and stark and bare
He hung his sign out anywhere.

"My doctrine is to lay aside
Contentions, and be satisfied.
Jest do your best, and praise er blame
That follows that, counts jest the same;
I've allus noticed great success
Is mixed with troubles, more or less;
And it's the man who does the best
That gets more kicks than all the rest."

But, when laboring for the upbuilding of the Master's kingdom, let come what will. Since our labor is one of love, let us go forward courageously and faithfully to the end; and whether we are called upon to walk joyfully or sorrowfully, let us keep close to Christ, doing all things as unto the Lord and not as unto men; seeing to it that no man take our crown. "Be thou faithful unto death, and I will give thee a crown of life."

From a human standpoint I believe that many ministers waste most of their time and that the money spent on them is wasted, because little appreciation is shown by those among whom they labor; and the results, viewed in human light, are so small that all is wasted. Yet, knowing as they do that even the waste places of the earth need the refreshing showers of Divine grace, and that the Gospel must be preached in all the world whether men will hear or forbear, and that their ministry is one of love, they labor on, leaving the results to God.

It is but natural that every minister should have some appreciation of his ability to occupy a position of prominence; and although believing that the valley of humiliation bears fairer fruit—fruit that has more of heaven's sweetness in it—than was ever grown on the hilltop of exaltation and praise, although reached by a laudable ambition success-fully realized, yet he would just as soon see other brethren in that fruitful valley. Let us remember what Anne of Austria, the Queen of France, said to her implacable enemy, Cardinal Richelieu: "My Lord-Cardinal, there is one fact which you seem to have entirely forgotten—God is a sure paymaster, He may not pay at the end of every week, month or year; but I charge you, remember that he pays in the end." Yes, the Savior has promised that the giving of a "cup of cold water only, in the name of a disciple, shall in no wise lose its reward."

The work some of God's laborers perform may be

very hard, and the pay very small, while the position they occupy is far from prominent in the eyes of their fellow men; but we believe that in that last great day, when the secrets of all hearts will be made known, and every man's work shall be tried by fire, and judged by One who is just as well as merciful, the assembled hosts before God's tribunal will acknowledge that there is no waste in the ministry of love, and the humblest worker in the Master's vineyard will be satisfied with the reward given.

God help us to realize that there is a gloriously bright side to His service now, and a great reward hereafter; and may the keynote to all that shall be done at this meeting of Synod be: No waste in the ministry of love. Daniel Webster said: "If we work upon marble, it will perish; if we work upon brass, time will efface it; if we rear temples, they will crumble into dust; but if we work upon immortal minds, if we imbue them with principles, with the just fear of God and love of our fellow men, we engrave on those tablets something which will brighten to all eternity."

"Now, the God of peace that brought again from the dead our Lord Jesus, that great Shepherd of the sheep, through the blood of the everlasting covenant, make you perfect in every good work to do His will, working in you that which is well pleasing in His sight, through Jesus Christ, to whom be glory forever and ever.   Amen.''

CHAPTER XLI

"Use every man after his desert, and who shall escape
whipping?"   —*Shakespeare.*

"The kindness of some is too much like an echo; it returns
exactly the counterpart of what it receives and neither more
nor less."   —*Bowes.*

During an exciting political campaign, when two
of our then noted politicians were stumping the
state, indulging in joint debate in the interests of
their respective parties in general and their own
interests in particular, these men decided that even
the remote San Juan should not be neglected.
Therefore, they staged it wherever the lines of Barlow & Sanderson would carry them; and where
there was no stage route they adopted the custom-
ary mode of travel (either horseback or on foot).
In this way the small camps at timber line were
reached and all had the privilege of hearing these
politicians debate on the issues of the day.

Notice was sent to Mineral Point, a camp at the
head of the Uncompahgre River, about eleven

jury and asked them to bring in a verdict as to the cause of their companion's death. This is the way the indignant judge explained matters to me. Said he: "What do you think the verdict was, Mr. Darley?" I had a good idea of what caused the man's death, but did not care to express my opinion in the matter. Then the judge, all excited, gave the shamefulness of the verdict, it being "Whisky." "Shameful," said he; "the young man has a fine mother and a nice sister living back East, and how could I write to them that the jury brought in a verdict of death by whisky?" So he talked straight to these men who had sworn to bring in a proper verdict, and told them they must try again. But after the second attempt to discover the cause of the man's death, nearly the same verdict was brought in as before. The judge waxed eloquent on the tenderness of the ties that bound the mother, brother and sister to the deceased. He appealed to the jury as to men who had some idea of the fitness of things, and asked how they would have liked such a verdict brought in about them had they died as their friend. The third time the verdict was correct—"heart failure." Then the judge said: "That is good; now I will write a nice letter to his mother and sister, and tell them what the verdict of the jury was; and they will never know the truth about his death."

As I looked into the face of this San Juan Justice of the Peace, Coroner, and a little of almost every thing, I felt that after all, this man, rough in appearance and willing to use his office to shield a friend, had a good quantity of the milk of human kindness in his heart. I knew the foreman of the jury, and therefore was a little surprised that he should allow a verdict in the first place that reflected on the character of the dead. But possibly there were conscientious scruples in the way. The jury were sworn to bring in a truthful verdict. However, in those days, friendship generally conquered and conscientious scruples gave way to surroundings. Men stood for their friends and defended their good names, whether they were alive or dead,

PERFECTION

"Perfection!"—God's goal in the distance,
  Far ahead of the best that we do;
'Way beyond our own lifelong endeavor,
  The goal never reached, though by few.

How, then, shall we offer our service
  To the One who is perfect and just?
How enter His presence rejoicing,
  And look to His mercy in trust?

Our efforts are feeble and falt'ring,
  Our prayers rise in blemish and doubt;
Our aims and our hopes are but weak ones;
  We turn not to face square about.

But Christ will present us all blameless
  Before Him the angels adore;
And His merits will gain us redemption,
  Though our service and spirit are poor.

For the work that we do for our Master,
  Though lacking in purpose and power,
Will be taken as worthy acceptance,
  Through Christ, and Calvary's hour.

PIONEERING IN THE SAN JUAN

Mistakes will happen most surely,
    And error will creep in unknown;
Yet Christ has made perfect atonement,
    And the Father still calls us His own.
                  —Rev. Geo. S. Darley.

"I will go forth 'mong men, not mailed in scorn,
But in the armor of a pure intent.
Great duties are before me, and great songs,
And whether crowned or crownless when I fall,
It matters not, so as God's work is done."
                  —Alexander Smith.

THE END

CPSIA information can be obtained
at www.ICGtesting.com
Printed in the USA
FFOW05n1657070114

9 781932 738612